THOMAS BERRY

The logo of the oak leaves is to recall the Great Red Oak at Thomas Berry's Riverdale Center for Religious Research.

MODERN SPIRITUAL MASTERS SERIES

THOMAS BERRY

Selected Writings on the Earth Community

Selected and
with an Introduction by

MARY EVELYN TUCKER

AND

JOHN GRIM

ORBIS BOOKS

Maryknoll, New York 10545

ORBIS BOOKS
Maryknoll, New York 10545

Fathers and Brothers
MARYKNOLL

Founded in 1970, Orbis Books endeavors to publish works that enlighten the mind, nourish the spirit, and challenge the conscience. The publishing arm of the Maryknoll Fathers and Brothers, Orbis seeks to explore the global dimensions of the Christian faith and mission, to invite dialogue with diverse cultures and religious traditions, and to serve the cause of reconciliation and peace. The books published reflect the views of their authors and do not represent the official position of the Maryknoll Society. To learn more about Maryknoll and Orbis Books, please visit our website at www.maryknollsociety.org.

Manufactured in the United States of America.

Berry, Thomas, 1914–2009.
  [Works. Selections]
    Selected Writings on the Earth Community / Thomas Berry ; selected and with an introduction by Mary Evelyn Tucker and John Grim.
      pages cm. (Modern spiritual masters)
    Includes bibliographical references.
    ISBN 978-1-62698-095-2 (pbk.)
    1. Ecotheology. 2. Theology. I. Tucker, Mary Evelyn. II. Grim, John. III. Title.
    B945.B4771 2014

    200–dc23   2014007908

To

Margaret Berry, Jean Berry Forester,
Ann Berry Somers, and Terry Kelleher,
who nurtured Thomas over many years

Contents

Sources

Books (in order of original date of publication)

Buddhism. New York: Columbia University Press, 1989 (orig. Anima Press, 1967).

Religions of India. New York: Columbia University Press, 1992 (orig. Anima Press, 1971).

The Dream of the Earth. San Francisco: Sierra Club Books, 1988. Excerpts copyright © 1988 by Thomas Berry. Used by permission of Sierra Club Books.

Befriending the Earth: A Theology of Reconciliation between Humans and the Earth (with Thomas Clark). Mystic, CT: Twenty-Third Publications, 1991.

The Universe Story with Brian Swimme. San Francisco: HarperSanFrancisco, 1992.

The Great Work: Our Way into the Future. New York: Harmony/Bell Tower, 1999.

Evening Thoughts: Reflecting on Earth as Sacred Community, edited by Mary Evelyn Tucker. San Francisco and Berkeley: Sierra Club and The University of California Press, 2006. Excerpts copyright © 2006 by Thomas Berry. Used by permission of Sierra Club Books.

The Sacred Universe: Earth, Spirituality, and Religion in the 21st Century, edited and with a foreword by Mary Evelyn Tucker. New York: Columbia University Press, 2009.

The Christian Future and the Fate of Earth, edited by Mary Evelyn Tucker and John Grim. Maryknoll, NY: Orbis Books, 2009.

Selected Monographs and Articles

"The New Story," *Teilhard Studies* no. 1, Anima Press, American Teilhard Association, Winter 1978.

"Management: The Managerial Ethos and the Future of Planet Earth," *Teilhard Studies* no. 3, Anima Press, American Teilhard Association, Spring 1980.

"Teilhard in the Ecological Age," *Teilhard Studies* no. 7, Anima Press, American Teilhard Association, Fall 1982.

"Technology and the Healing of the Earth," *Teilhard Studies,* no. 14, Anima Press, American Teilhard Association, Fall 1985.

"Alienation in a Universe of Presence," *Teilhard Studies* no. 48, American Teilhard Association, Spring 2004.

"Individualism and Holism in Chinese Traditions: The Religious Cultural Context," in *Confucian Spirituality,* edited by Tu Weiming and Mary Evelyn Tucker, New York: Crossroad, 2003.

Acknowledgments

We are grateful for invaluable assistance in preparing this manuscript from Matt Riley, who embodies Berry's Great Work. In addition, we wish to extend our gratitude to Christy Riley, Donald St. John, Susan Wigler, and Judy Emery. We give deep thanks to Tara Trapani, who has been indispensable in overseeing the numerous details for publication, amidst many other demands.

We remember especially our fellow graduate students at Fordham and the American Teilhard Association members, who supported Thomas for many years at Riverdale. We celebrate as well our friendship with Brian Thomas Swimme, Miriam MacGillis, Brian Brown, Kimie and Tatsuhiko Watanabe, Terry Tempest Williams, Julianne Warren, Kathleen Dean Moore, and most especially our friends from Minnesota, Bucknell, and from Oxford days, who have sustained us in this work more than they can imagine.

Introduction

Thomas Berry:
Living a New Story

Thomas Berry was an original and prophetic voice for the Earth community.[1] As a gifted speaker, an original thinker, and an inspiring teacher, he reshaped our thinking about human-Earth relations. Drawing on his broad knowledge of world religions and his deep feeling for the journey of the universe, he identified "story" as a means of guiding humans into the future.

Berry was born on November 9, 1914, in Greensboro, North Carolina, where he spent his early childhood and where he returned when he was eighty. It was there that he died peacefully on June 1, 2009, and was buried at Green Mountain Monastery in Vermont. Named William Nathan after his father, he was the third child of thirteen of which four siblings remain. He entered the Passionist Order with a desire to read, reflect, and contemplate. Upon ordination he took the name Thomas after Thomas Aquinas, whose writings he admired, especially the *Summa Theologica*.

After completing his doctorate from Catholic University with a thesis on Giambattista Vico, he studied in China from 1948 to 1949. There he met Wm. Theodore de Bary who was to become a lifelong friend and one of the most renowned Asian scholars in the West. Along with his wife, Fanny, Ted was among Berry's earliest supporters. During many an evening at their home in Tappan, New York, Thomas and Ted would discuss the spiritual

dimensions of the Asian classics, especially Confucianism. Fanny
shared Berry's interest in Pierre Teilhard de Chardin (1881–
1955) and always assisted at the annual meetings of the American Teilhard Association in New York. At Columbia University,
Ted established a groundbreaking Asian studies program highlighting the classical texts and the history of India, China, and
Japan. He also founded an Asian Thought and Religion Seminar
along with Berry. Theirs was a rich and sustaining friendship at
a time when few understood Berry's keen interest in Asian religions. Berry authored two books on Asian religions, *Buddhism*
(1967) and *Religions of India* (1971), which are still in print
with Columbia University Press.

From 1975 to 1987, Berry served as president of the American Teilhard Association. In 1978, Berry initiated the *Teilhard
Studies* series with his essay, "The New Story: Comments on
the Origin, Identification and Transmission of Values." Here
he called for the articulation of a new story of evolution and
the emergence of life. The work of Teilhard de Chardin was a
major inspiration for Berry in developing his ideas for a universe story, especially Teilhard's feeling for the great sweep of
evolution from lesser to greater complexity and consciousness. This perspective was also a context for Berry's ecological
concerns.

Berry was an outspoken advocate for the environment. Early
on, he called for the restitution of habitat for biodiversity, not
simply as a conservation measure, but in recognition of the
intrinsic value of nature. His vision of a flourishing Earth community gave him an unparalleled drive. In fact, some of his
most insightful writing and publications occurred after he was
sixty-five and had retired from teaching. This included *The
Dream of the Earth* in 1988, *The Great Work* in 1999, and
Evening Thoughts in 2006. *The Christian Future and the Fate
of Earth* along with *The Sacred Universe* were published in
2009, the year he died.

THOMAS BERRY AS SCHOLAR, TEACHER, AND MENTOR

Berry began his teaching at Seton Hall University in New Jersey from 1956 to 1961 and then taught from 1961 to 1965 at St. John's University on Long Island. In 1966, the Jesuit Christopher Mooney invited him to come to Fordham University to teach in the theology department. There he founded and directed the History of Religions program before retiring from teaching in 1979. This was the only program of its kind at any Catholic university in North America. During his tenure, Berry trained some twenty-five doctoral students, many of whom are teaching at major colleges and universities in the United States and Canada.

Berry was an anomaly in Fordham's theology department. He was neither a Jesuit, nor a theologian. Instead, he was trained in Western history and in world religions. As a charismatic figure and an engaging speaker, he drew students to the History of Religions program, in fact more than any other section in the theology department. Students came from around the country, some turning down admission to religious studies programs at Columbia or Yale to study with him.

It was an exhilarating time for students to study with this brilliant thinker and generous mentor. Having read widely in world religions and learned the languages needed to appreciate their ancient texts and commentaries, Berry set a high bar. They thrived on the challenges he presented: namely, learn the textual language of at least one tradition, know the history of many, appreciate the spiritual wisdom of each tradition, and read widely in an interdisciplinary fashion so that the living context of a tradition might open up.

Berry's appreciation for the wisdom of world religions was legendary. Well before interreligious dialogue became a topic for discussion, he was immersing himself in the texts and traditions of India, China, and Japan. In addition, he had a great appreciation for Native American and indigenous traditions. Following the Vatican II document, *Nostra Aetate*, that spoke of the "rays of Truth" available from world religions, he observed that, indeed, these traditions held not just rays of truth but floods of illumination.

While teaching at Fordham, Berry founded the Riverdale Center for Religious Research along the Hudson River, which he directed for twenty-five years from 1970 to 1995. The Center was located in a rambling old Victorian house where Berry arranged his extensive library of some ten thousand books. These consisted of the primary texts of the world religions as well as commentaries on these texts. Many of these scriptures were in the original languages—the Hebrew Bible, the Latin Church Fathers, the Arabic Qu'ran, as well as the Sanskrit texts of Hinduism and Buddhism, and the Chinese classics of Confucianism and Daoism. In addition, Berry had a room upstairs devoted to Native American traditions. Students came to the Center to do research, get advice on their dissertations, or simply talk about current affairs. On the first Saturday of each month during the academic year, there were gatherings of students and a broader public to hear a talk and enjoy a potluck dinner. Berry attracted a great variety of intellectuals and environmentalists from the New York area and beyond. The welcoming atmosphere of the Center led to lifelong friendships formed around the creative ideas Berry was beginning to articulate.

CALLS FOR
AN AWAKENING AND EXODUS

It was during this period in the 1970s that Berry began to be keenly aware of a variety of environmental problems: from pollution of air, soil, and water to unbridled consumption and biodiversity loss. What is particularly remarkable is how early Berry understood the magnitude and complexity of these issues. While many ignored his warnings over thirty years ago, now his insights about the religious character of the environmental crisis continue to be prescient. Indeed, in a tribute to Berry, the noted process theologian, John Cobb, observed, "No other writer in the ecological movement has had analogous effectiveness" in helping us realize the "radical uniqueness of this crisis."[2]

He raised penetrating questions regarding the lateness and laxity of the response from the major establishments of our time—educational, political, religious, and economic. In this spirit, Berry strongly challenged world religions to respond appropriately to the growing environmental crisis. Above all, he focused his critique on the religious establishments as the transmitters of ancient wisdom traditions that had been shaped by cosmological concerns that were embedded in human-nature interactions. Why, he wondered, have religions been blind to the fate of Earth? Is this because the desire for personal salvation from a flawed material world into a heavenly realm supersedes all other concerns? In other words, does the search for other-worldly rewards override commitment to this world? Has the material order of nature been devalued by religious transcendence? Have human-centered ethics been so all-consuming that we now do not have an ethics that addresses such impending collective acts as ecocide and biocide? Did religions surrender their interest in natural theology and cosmology to science? These questions required further reflection, he suggested, before an adequate response to our situation can be formulated from out of any one religious tradition.

Indeed, Berry reopens a gateway for the religions to reform their traditions by drawing on the metaphor of "exodus" proposed by the historian Eric Voegelin. Berry realized that world religions were being called to make an exodus passage from their traditional worldviews into the modern world. Like the exodus experience of the Jews out of Egypt, Berry called religions to make a transition into modernity. However, religions have found this transition challenging and thus often revert to fundamentalism. In critiquing the ineffectual response of religious institutions and seminaries to the environmental crisis, he also suggested that it is not too late. It is more important than ever that these institutions reflect on their cosmological depth and their past interactions with local bioregions as they become involved in current environmental issues. Having prepared themselves, religious practitioners and leaders alike can make their contributions—in universities, in seminaries, in religious settings, and in grassroots movements. This was part of the inspiration for the Harvard conference series on World Religions and Ecology in which Berry participated from 1996 to 1998. In addition, it orients the ongoing work of the Forum on Religion and Ecology at Yale (see www.yale.edu/religionandecology).

More and more, religious communities are drawing on Berry's ideas and others, as they write statements on the environment, create liturgies, form eco-communities, organize study groups, and get involved in ecological issues. This has been especially true of the religious orders of nuns in the United States, Canada, Ireland, England, and Australia. Many of them have been inspired by the talks of the Dominican sister Miriam MacGillis, who has spread Berry's ideas widely. Working closely with him, she founded an eco-learning center and community-supported garden at Genesis Farm in 1980. In that same period, the Catholic Bishops of the Philippines, influenced by Berry, issued a pastoral letter on the environment entitled "What Is Happening to Our Beautiful Land?" (1988). Two decades later, in December 2008, they published another statement listing the critical environmental problems their country is still facing and called for a moratorium on mining and logging. In February 2009, the Catholic Bishop of Alberta, Canada, wrote a strong condemnation of the oil extraction from tar sands, noting that such widespread environmental destruction is morally reprehensible.

THE INFLUENCE OF THOMAS AQUINAS AND TEILHARD DE CHARDIN

Thomas Berry acknowledged that the promise inherent in the religions for ecological awareness still has to be fully recognized and articulated. He spoke, for example, of the deep appreciation for the order and beauty of Creation contained in the Christian tradition ranging from the Psalms to the visionary prayers of

Francis of Assisi, the cosmology of Thomas Aquinas in the medieval period, and the cosmological vision of Pierre Teilhard de Chardin in the twentieth century.

A central influence on Berry was Aquinas's cosmological emphasis on the participation of all reality in God's being. In addition, he was influenced by Aquinas's reworking of Aristotle's view that abstract concepts depend on specific existing material reality. This affirmation of matter also had its mystical side that Berry described in terms taken directly from Aquinas, namely, the cosmological dimension of every being. This mystical view can be traced back to the early Christian writer of the third century identified as Pseudo-Dionysius. He spoke of a form of ineffable knowing described as "divine rays of darkness." Aquinas's position, however, is that all things go forth from God into the material world and return to God. This situates human knowing not simply as abstract, but as shaped by interaction and participation in material reality. Thus, Aquinas preserved the creative tension between an inner, immanent direction, or form, within matter itself, and the transcendent cosmological source of the originating impulse of creation.

In addition to Aquinas, Berry drew increasingly on the thought of Pierre Teilhard de Chardin for insight into the story of our times, namely, the emerging, evolutionary universe. Teilhard provided a large-scale vision of humans as situated within the vast context of cosmic evolution. He had a profound sense of the increasing complexity and consciousness of evolution from the molecular to the cellular, and from multi-cellular organisms to the explosion of diverse life forms. Teilhard's major work titled *The Human Phenomenon* (first published in 1960) was for Berry a powerful narration of universe emergence. While Teilhard saw his work as science, Berry narrated it as a story. Berry's 1978 essay on "The New Story" was republished in his first collection of essays in 1988, *The Dream of the Earth*. This collection showed the influence of Teilhard but also his own independent thinking regarding the environment.

Rather than settling on Teilhard's insights, Berry pushed beyond to explore the conjunction of cosmology and ecology. While appreciating Teilhard, he also critiqued his optimistic view of "building the Earth" with new technologies and scientific discoveries. He balanced Teilhard's technological optimism with a strong sense of ecological realism—highlighting our current patterns of environmental degradation. He wanted us to see that in a geological instant we were diminishing the life of ecosystems, rivers, and oceans. Our historical moment, he would observe, was as significant as the change implied in a geological era.

THE ECOZOIC ERA

Reaching into his own past in North Carolina, Berry recalled his boyhood experience of a summer meadow filled with white lilies. This experience began to define his commitment to preserve and protect such beauty. Increasingly he spoke of a deep affectivity and authenticity imparted by Earth itself in its biodiversity. It was in the early 1980s that these ideas coalesced in his term "Ecozoic." This was his way of marking the end of a geological era in which thousands of species were disappearing each year amidst the industrial-technological bubble of resource extraction. He observed that scientists were telling us that we are in the midst of an extinction period. Nothing this devastating had occurred since the dinosaurs went extinct sixty-five million years ago and the Cenozoic era began. But rather than leaving his audience in despair, he used the term "Ecozoic" to name that emerging period in which humans would recover their creative orientation to Earth.

Within this broad context, he had an insight into his own role in reflecting on these issues. Flying back from an environmental conference in the Seychelle Islands, looking down over the Nile River at thirty thousand feet, he realized that he was not a theologian, but rather a "geologian." With this term, he viewed himself as a human being who emerged out of eons of Earth's geological and biological evolution and was now reflecting on our world. This reflection was a way to reinvent the human at the species level.

The notion of reinventing the role of the human was enhanced when, in 1982, Berry met Brian Swimme, who came to the Riverdale Center for a year of study. Having earned a doctorate in mathematical cosmology at the University of Oregon, Brian was the ideal partner for collaboration. Berry's years of study of world history and religions was paralleled by Brian's comprehensive study of evolutionary history. They engaged in an intense, decade-long collaboration including research, lectures, and conferences. From this there emerged the jointly authored book, *The Universe Story,* in 1992. This was the first time the history of evolution was told as a story in which humans have a critical role.

It was nearly two decades later that the *Journey of the Universe* film was completed, also inspired by the need for a new narrative of the epic of evolution. This was the first time the story was told in film, accompanied by a book and a series of interviews with scientists and historians, educators, and environmentalists. *Journey of the Universe* is profoundly indebted to Berry's thinking on evolution, ecology, and spirituality.

CONCLUSION

The layers of Berry's thinking are multiple and have organic continuity with one another. Among these layers are the following: the play of texts, institutions, and personalities in the history of religions; the cultural-historical settings in which religions emerge and develop; the inherent and formative relationships of local bioregions and indigenous societies; the complex relations between and among world religions; cosmological expressions within the various religions; the awakening to our growing realization of the continuity of the human with the community of life; the evolutionary story as a functional cosmology for our multicultural planetary civilization. All of these are set within his concern for the fate of the Earth community and his desire to evoke mutually enhancing human-Earth relations.

As a storyteller, Berry guided his listeners into the power and engagement of historical studies in religious cultures and civilizations. Like all storytellers, Berry had an intuitive sense of his own rhetorical power, but unlike many storytellers, he did not simply rely on emotional rhetoric or the large gesture. Drawing out his syllables in a laconic North Carolinian manner, he would calmly elucidate complex topics that truly engaged him. This reflective style enabled him to ponder both the problematic story of our industrial age, as well as the recovery of human energy and the reinvention of the human spirit.

Loving humor and fond of a trickster's play in the transformative character of life, Berry was academically formed before the postmodern penchant for uncovering power dynamics and concealing rhetoric. Still, he was alert to interactions in which individuals participated in larger civilizations and cosmologies by active understanding, intuitive glimpses, and disciplined effort. Story, then, for Berry was not simply passive reception by a listener, but an engaged, participatory event in which the story was present and alive in the telling.

In all these reflections, there remains the image of Berry in his brown corduroy jacket, lecturing in public or in class, articulating with wonder, beauty, and creativity his dream of the Earth community fully embodied.

1

The Story of the Universe

"The New Story" is a culmination of a lifetime of Berry's reflections on the growing ecological crisis and what new paradigm would be essential to counteract the devastating power of extractive industries and consumer economies. This new story, he felt, could begin to break through the modern view of materialism and reductionism that had objectified nature primarily as a resource for human use.

To do this he felt we needed a coherent evolutionary story that would draw together science and religion in an integrated manner. Recognizing the immense complexities of both science and religion, he nonetheless felt that a fresh creative integration of the two was critical for our times. In other words, the revolutions of the last three centuries in astronomy with Copernicus, gravitation with Newton, genetics with Mendel, biology with Darwin, and physics with Einstein could be threaded together in an epic story of evolution. Moreover, the more recent discoveries regarding the unfolding of the early universe needed to be told in a way that was comprehensible and comprehensive. Thus the new cosmology of universe emergence and the formation of stars and galaxies could now be told in a manner that was accessible to a nonscientist. Moreover, the new understanding of planetary formation and the emergence of life on Earth could be narrated in a way that the viewer could recognize the evolutionary processes of both universe and Earth as dynamic, differentiating, and self-organizing.

All of this is to say that humans have emerged out of these processes and are not an addendum to them. Rather they are the self-reflective consciousness of Earth itself. We are related to all other species, sharing their genetic coding. Moreover, we see the stars, too, as our ancestors for out of their explosions have come the elements necessary for life.

Berry was thus concerned to see the evolutionary story as a unifying epic that would ignite an awareness of our deep connection with the universe and Earth and our place as a species among other species. This sweeping cosmological narrative could provide a cosmological context for an ecological ethic of reverence, respect, and restraint toward Earth and its myriad life forms.

One of Berry's central convictions was that as we began to see the universe as an unfolding symphony and Earth as a living planet, we would be able to find our role as participants in these dynamic processes. As we appreciate the immense diversity of the Earth community, we would come more fully into communion with Earth's ecosystems and life forms. Thus, learning to work with nature's creativity would become our "Great Work" in the newly emerging ecological age that Berry called the Ecozoic era.

"The New Story" was written in 1978 when Berry was sixty-four. This essay was the inspiration for The Universe Story, *which Berry published with Brian Swimme in 1992 after a decade-long collaboration. It was also a major inspiration for* Journey of the Universe *(2011), which Brian wrote with Mary Evelyn Tucker during a dozen years of working together on the film and book.*

THE NEW STORY

It's all a question of story. We are in trouble just now because we do not have a good story. We are in between stories. The old story, the account of how the world came to be and how we fit into it, is no longer effective. Yet we have not learned the new story. Our traditional story of the universe sustained us for a long period of time. It shaped our emotional attitudes, provided us with life purposes, and energized action. It consecrated suffering and integrated knowledge. We awoke in the morning and knew where we were. We could answer the questions of our children. We could identify crime, punish transgressors. Everything was taken care of because the story was there. It did not necessarily make people good, nor did it take away the pains and stupidities of life or make for unfailing warmth in human association. It did provide a context in which life could function in a meaningful manner.

Presently this traditional story is dysfunctional in its larger social dimensions, even though some believe it firmly and act according to its guidance. Aware of the dysfunctional aspects of the traditional program, some persons have moved on into different, often new-age, orientations, which have consistently proved ineffective in dealing with our present life situation. Even with advanced science and technology, with superb techniques in manufacturing and commerce, in communications and computation, our secular society remains without satisfactory meaning or the social discipline needed for a life leading to emotional, aesthetic, and spiritual fulfillment. Because of this lack of satisfaction, many persons are returning to a religious fundamentalism. But that, too, can be seen as inadequate to supply the values for sustaining our needed social discipline.

A radical reassessment of the human situation is needed, especially concerning those basic values that give to life some satisfactory meaning. We need something that will supply our times what was supplied formerly by our traditional religious story. If we are to achieve this purpose, we must begin where everything begins in human affairs—with the basic story, our narrative of how things came to be, how they came to be as they are, and how the future can be given some satisfying direction. We need a story that will educate us, a story that will heal, guide, and discipline us.

Western society did have, in its traditional story of the universe, an agreed-upon functioning story up until somewhere around the fourteenth century. This religion-based story originated in a revelatory experience some three thousand years ago. According to this story, the original harmony of the universe was broken by a primordial human fault, and that necessitated formation of a believing redemptive community that would take shape through the course of time. Human history was moving infallibly toward its fulfillment in the peace of a reconstituted paradise.

This religious story was integrated with the Ptolemaic account of the universe and how it functioned, an abiding universe that endlessly renewed itself and its living forms through the seasonal sequence of time. The introduction of irreversible historical time onto this abiding cosmological scene is precisely the contribution of the Western religious tradition. However severe the turbulent moments of history through the late classical and early medieval periods, these at least took place within a secure natural world and within a fixed context of interpretation. Whatever the problems were, they were not problems concerning the basic human or spiritual values that were at stake. Those were clear. . . .

The story of the universe is the story of the emergence of a galactic system in which each new level of expression emerges through the urgency of self-transcendence. Hydrogen in the presence of some millions of degrees of heat emerges into helium. After the stars take shape as oceans of fire in the heavens, they go through a sequence of transformations. Some eventually explode into the stardust out of which the solar system and the planet Earth take shape. Earth gives unique expression of itself in its rock and crystalline structures and in the variety and splendor of living forms, until humans appear as the moment in which the unfolding universe becomes conscious of itself. The human emerges not only as an Earthling, but also as a worldling. We bear the universe in our beings as the universe bears us in its being. The two have a total presence to each other and to that deeper mystery out of which both the universe and ourselves have emerged.

If this integral vision is something new both to the scientist and to the believer, both are gradually becoming aware of this view of the real and its human meaning. It might be considered a new revelatory experience. Because we are moving into a new mythic age, it is little wonder that a kind of mutation is taking place in the entire Earth-human order. A new paradigm of what it is to be human emerges. This is what is so exciting, yet so painful and so disrupting. One aspect of this change involves the shift in Earth-human relations, for we now in large measure determine the Earth process that once determined us. In a more integral way, we could say that the planet Earth that controlled itself directly in the former period now to an extensive degree controls itself through us.

In this new context, the question appears as to where the values are, how they are determined, and how they are transmitted. Whereas formerly values consisted in the perfection of the Earthly image reflecting an external Logos in a world of fixed natures, values are now determined by the human sensitivity in responding to the creative urgencies of a developing world. The scientist in the depths of the unconscious is drawn by the mystical attraction of communion with the emerging creative process. This would not be possible unless it were a call of subject to subject, if it were not an effort at total self-realization on the part of the scientists. As scientists, their taste for the real is what gives to their work its admirable quality. Their wish is to experience the real in its tangible, opaque, material aspect and to respond to that by establishing an interaction with the world that will advance the total process. If the demand for objectivity and the quantitative aspect of the real has led scientists to neglect subjectivity and the qualitative aspect of the real, this has been until now a condition for fulfilling their historical task. The most notable single development within science in recent years, however, has been a growing awareness of the integral physical-psychic dimension of reality. . . .

It is of utmost importance that succeeding generations become aware of the larger story outlined here and the numinous, sacred values that have been present in an expanding sequence over this entire time of the world's existence. Within this context all our human affairs—all professions, occupations, and activities—have their meaning precisely insofar as they enhance this emerging world of subjective intercommunion within the total range of reality. Within this context the scientific community and the religious community have a common basis. The limitations of the redemption rhetoric and the scientific rhetoric can be seen, and a new, more integral language of being and value can emerge.

Within this story, a structure of knowledge can be established, with its human significance, from the physics of the universe and its chemistry through geology and biology to economics and commerce and so to all those studies whereby we fulfill our role in the Earth process. There is no way of guiding the course of human affairs through the perilous course of the future except by discovering our role in this larger evolutionary process. If the way of Western civilization and Western religion was once the way of election and differentiation from others and from Earth, the way now is the way of intimate communion with the larger human community and with the universe itself.

Here we might observe that the basic mood of the future might well be one of confidence in the continuing revelation that takes place in and through Earth. If the dynamics of the universe from the beginning shaped the course of the heavens, lighted the sun, and formed Earth, if this same dynamism brought forth the continents and seas and atmosphere, if it awakened life in the primordial cell and then brought into being the unnumbered variety of living beings, and finally brought us into being and guided us safely through the turbulent centuries, there is reason to believe that this same guiding process is precisely what has awakened in us our present understanding of ourselves and our relation to this stupendous process. Sensitized to such guidance from the very structure and functioning of the universe, we can have confidence in the future that awaits the human venture.

—"The New Story," in *The Dream of the Earth,*
123–25, 132–33, 136–37

THE DREAM OF THE EARTH

This story of the past provides our most secure basis of hope that Earth will so guide us through the peril of the present that we may provide a fitting context for the next phase of the emergent mystery of earthly existence. That the guidance is available we cannot doubt. The difficulty is in the order of magnitude of change that is required of us. We have become so acclimated to an industrial world that we can hardly imagine any other context of survival even when we recognize that the industrial bubble is dissolving and will soon leave us in the chill of a plundered landscape.

None of our former revelatory experiences, none of our renewal or rebirth rituals, none of our apocalyptic descriptions are quite adequate for this moment. Their mythic power remains in a context far removed from the power that is abroad in our world. But even as we glance over the grimy world before us, the sun shines radiantly over planet Earth, the aspen leaves shimmer in the evening breeze, the coo of the Mourning Dove and the swelling chorus of the insects fill the land, while down in the hollows the mist deepens the fragrance of the honeysuckle. Soon the late summer moon will give a light sheen to the landscape. Something of a dream experience. Perhaps on occasion we participate in the original dream of Earth. Perhaps there are times when this primordial design becomes visible, as in a palimpsest, when we remove the later imposition. The dream of Earth. Where else can we go for the guidance needed for the task that is before us.

—"The Cosmology of Peace," in
The Dream of the Earth, 222–23

THE HUMAN AS INTEGRAL
WITH THE UNIVERSE

With all the inadequacies of any narrative, the epic of evolution does present the story of the universe as this story is now available to us out of our present experience. This is our sacred story. . . .

To appreciate the numinous aspect of the universe as this is communicated in this story, we need to understand that we ourselves activate one of the deepest dimensions of the universe. We can recognize in ourselves our special intellectual, emotional, and imaginative capacities. That these capacities have existed as dimensions of the universe from its beginning is clear since the universe is ever integral with itself in all its manifestations throughout its vast extension in space and throughout the sequence of its transformations in time. The human is neither an addendum nor an intrusion into the universe. We are quintessentially integral with the universe.

In ourselves the universe is revealed to itself as we are revealed in the universe. Such a statement could be made about any aspect of the universe because every being in the universe articulates some special quality of the universe in its entirety. Indeed, nothing in the universe could be itself apart from every other being in the universe, nor could any moment of the universe story exist apart from all the other moments in the story. Yet it is within our own being that we have our own unique experience of the universe and of Earth in its full reality.

—"The Earth Story," in *The Great Work*, 31–32

THE UNIVERSE AS SYMPHONY

This sensitive experience of the universe and of the planet Earth leads us to appreciate the ten billion years required for the universe to bring Earth into existence and another four billion years for Earth to shape itself in such splendor. For our present Earth is not Earth as it always was and always will be. It is Earth at a highly developed phase in its continuing emergence. We need to see the sequence of earthly transformations as so many movements in a musical composition. In music, the earlier notes are gone when the later notes are played, but the musical phrase, indeed the entire symphony, needs to be heard simultaneously. We do not fully understand the opening notes until the later notes are heard. Each new theme alters the meaning of the earlier themes and the entire composition. The opening theme resonates throughout all the later parts of the piece.

Thus the origin moment of the universe presents us with a stupendous process that we begin to appreciate in its magnificence as it unfolds through the ages. The flaring forth of the primordial energy carried within itself all that would ever happen in the long series of transformations that would bring the universe into its present mode of being. The original moment of the universe in its primordial energies contained the undetermined possibilities of the present, just as the present is the activation of these possibilities. This primordial emergence was the beginning of Earth's story as well as the beginning of the personal story of each of us, since the story of the universe is the story of each individual being in the universe. Indeed, the reality inherent in the beginning could not be known until the shaping forces held in this process had brought forth the galaxies, Earth, its multitude of living species, and the reflection of the universe on itself in human intelligence.

After the universe's origin moment, a sequence of other transformational moments took place: the shaping of the first-generation stars within their various galaxies, then the supernova collapse of first-generation stars. These creative moments brought into being the entire array of elements. These in turn made possible the future developments throughout the universe, especially on the planet Earth, where the expansion of life needed the broad spectrum of elements for its full development.

The gravitational attractions functioning throughout the universe gathered the scattered stardust into this second-generation star we call our sun, and surrounding this star, its eight planets. Within this context, Earth began its distinctive self-expression, a groping toward its unknowable and unpredictable future, yet carrying within itself a tendency toward greater differentiation, a deepening subjectivity, and a more intimate self-bonding of its component parts.

Such wonder comes over us as we reflect on the planet Earth finding its proper distance from the sun so that it would be

neither too hot nor too cold, shaping its radius so that it would
be neither too large (and thus make Earth more gaseous, like
Jupiter) nor too small (and thus make Earth more arid and rocky,
like Mars). Then the Earth-moon distance was established so
precisely—the moon was neither too close that the tides would
overwhelm the continents nor so distant that the seas would be
stagnant and life could not emerge.

—"The Gaia Hypothesis: Its Religious Implications,"
in *The Sacred Universe*, 107–9

A LIVING PLANET

Profound mysteries were taking place all this while, the most
mysterious of which was this setting into place of the conditions required for the emergence of life and human consciousness. Principally through the work of James Lovelock and Lynn
Margulis, we now understand in some detail that the story of
life is so bound up with the story of Earth's geological structure
that we can no longer think of Earth as first taking shape in
its full physical form and then life somehow emerging within
this context. The simultaneous shaping of its physical form and
the shaping of its life took place in intimate association with
each other. The living forms that appeared in the early history of
Earth were among the most powerful forces shaping the atmosphere, the hydrosphere, and even the geological structures of
the planet.

But while we need to understand the shaping power of living
forms in the sequence of Earth's transformations, we must understand that living forms themselves were brought into being by
the shaping power of earlier Earth development. Always there is
this integral relationship between the earlier and the later. In the
larger arc of this transformation process, the simpler forms are
earlier, the most complex forms later, just as the simpler atomic
elements took shape in the earliest moments of the universe and
the more complex elements came later.

Much else might be said about this early phase of Earth's development, yet it is sufficient to note that each of these early occurrences in the life development of the planet were decisive. Each had to happen at precisely the opportune moment in the sequence of Earth's development for the planet to be what it presently is.

While perhaps incomplete, the narrative as given here presents in outline the story of the universe and of the planet Earth as this story is now available to us. This is our sacred story. It is our way of dealing with the ultimate mystery whence all things come into being. It is much more than an account of matter and its random emergence into the visible world about us, because the emergent process, as indicated by the geneticist Theodosius Dobzhansky (1900–1975), is neither random nor determined, but creative, just as in the human order creativity is neither a rational, deductive process nor an irrational wandering of the undisciplined mind, but the emergence of beauty as mysteriously as the blossoming of a field of daisies out of the dark earth.

On Earth we find the fulfillment of the primordial tendency of the universe toward clearly articulated and highly differentiated entities. Earth astounds us with the vast differences between itself and the other planets. Each of the planets has its own distinctive mode of being, but these other planets are all much more like one another than any of them are like Earth.

This unique mode of Earth-being is expressed primarily in the number and diversity of living forms that exist on Earth, living forms so integral to one another and with the structure and functioning of the planet that we can appropriately speak of Earth as a "Living Planet." This term is used neither literally nor simply metaphorically, but as analogy, somewhat similar in its structure to the analogy expressed when we say that we "see," an expression used primarily for physical sight but also used to connote intellectual understanding. A proportional relationship is expressed. The eye is to what it experiences as the intellect is to what it experiences. The common quality is that of subjective presence of one form to another as distinctly other. In this experience, the identity of each is enhanced, not diminished.

So in using this term "living" in speaking about a tree as a living being and in speaking about Earth as a living being, we are indicating that some of the basic aspects of life, such as the capacity for inner homeostasis amid the diversity of external conditions, are found proportionately realized both in the tree and in the comprehensive functioning of the planet. In the tree, as the primary analogue, we have the basic functioning of the life process through its beginning as a seed with its identifiable genetic coding, its absorption of the energies of the sun, and the flow of nourishment from its roots through its trunk to its leaves. Then there is the process of self-reproduction through its seeds. This process produces a certain continuing transformation of the surrounding atmosphere, whereby the presence of the life process can be discerned.

So too Earth comes into being. Not, however, with an identifiable genetic coding guiding Earth through its stages of development to its maturity nor through birth from a prior Earth or living organism with the capacity to continue this generative process. Earth cannot reproduce itself. Yet notwithstanding, there are similarities that justify the use of the term "living" to describe Earth in its integral functioning, especially in its capacity for inner self-adjustment to the diversity of external conditions to which it is subject. This "feedback" process is so remarkable that, along with the capacity of the planet to bring forth such an abundance of life forms, Earth can be described not simply as living but as living in a supereminent manner.

The use of metaphor and analogy does not diminish the reality of what is being said. The more primordial realities can only be spoken of in a symbolic manner. To indicate that Earth is not exactly a living reality in the sense that a bird or a flower is a living reality is not to diminish the significance of Earth as a living being. It is rather to heighten the significance of what we are saying. Earth makes possible all those multiple forms of life upon the planet, not simply some single life form. Earth "flowers" into the immense variety of species, not simply into another Earth.

The deepest mystery of all this is surely the manner in which these forms of life, from the plankton in the sea and the bacteria in the soil to the giant sequoia or to the most massive mammals, are ultimately related to one another in the comprehensive bonding of all the life systems. Genetically speaking, every living being is coded not only in regard to its own interior processes, but in relation to the entire complex of earthly being. This is to be alive and to be the fertile source of life.

—"The Gaia Hypothesis: Its Religious Implications," in
The Sacred Universe, 109–12

NEW FORMS OF RELIGIOUS ENCHANTMENT

For the human especially, the multiple modes of our being require both the activation of the physical and biological modes of being and the activation of the psychic mode of our being. We have our individual self, our biological self, our Earth self, and our universe self. It is through attraction to the larger modes of our self that we are drawn so powerfully toward our experience of Earth. We seek to travel throughout Earth, to see everything, to experience the grandeur of the mountains, to plunge into the sea, to raft the rivers, to fly through the air, even to go beyond Earth into space. We seek this for the expansion of our being, even more than for the physical thrill. In all these experiences we come to know the further realms of ourselves and experience the deepest mysteries of existence—what might well be considered the numinous origins whence the planet Earth and the entire universe derive, subsist, and have their highest mode of fulfillment.

Thus the scientist seeks to understand Earth in all its geological and biological forms, to examine the inner realms of the atomic and subatomic worlds. Even recent concerns for understanding

Earth as a living organism arise not from an arbitrary feeling that it would be an interesting venture of the human mind. We are, rather, impelled to this inquiry through our efforts at our own self-discovery. It is a mystical venture, for its ultimate purpose is to achieve a final communion with that ultimate reality whence all things come into being. The dedication of personal effort, the life discipline, the excitement of the discoveries made, the differences, the identities, the coherences, the moments of intellectual impasse—all these reveal a new form of religious enchantment and a quest for further revelatory experience. For the universe whence we emerged is constantly calling us back to itself. So too Earth is calling us back to itself, and not only to us but to all its components, calling them into an intimacy with one another and to the larger community within which all earthly realities have their existence. . . .

Indeed, our scientific inquiry in this direction establishes the basis for a new type of religious experience different from but profoundly related to the religious-spiritual experience of the earlier shamanic period in human history. Since religious experience emerges from a sense of the awesome aspects of the natural world, our religious consciousness is consistently related to a cosmology that tells us the story of how things came to be in the beginning, how they came to be as they are, and the role of the human in enabling the universe in its earthly manifestation to continue the mysterious course of its creative self-expression.

—"The Gaia Hypothesis: Its Religious Implications," in
The Sacred Universe, 113–16

DIVERSITY AND UNITY

From a religious perspective, we might consider that because of the diversity of life expression that is held together in such intimate unity, Earth is a special presentation of the deep mysteries of existence whence religious consciousness arises. Thomas Aquinas refers to "difference" as "the perfection of the universe." The reason is that the divine could not imagine itself in any single being, so the divine brought into being an immense variety of beings. Thus the perfection lacking to one would be supplied by the others. "Consequently, the whole universe together participates in the divine goodness more perfectly, and manifests it better than any single being whatever" (Thomas Aquinas, *Summa Theologica* 1.47.1).

We could adapt this passage by simply saying that the deep mysteries of existence are manifested more perfectly in accord with the greater diversity held in the greater unity. This provides us with a way of dealing with the special role of Earth as revealing the deepest realms of existence with a perfection unequalled in any other mode of being we know of. For on Earth we have our most magnificent display of diversity caught up into the coherence of an unparalleled unity.

In this context, we can understand the special numinous quality attributed to Earth. In its own self-manifestation, Earth is also a revelation of the ultimate mystery of things. The sense of awe and mystery that was evoked in the earliest human awakening to the universe is beginning to awaken once more within this new context of scientific understanding. We have indeed lost contact with the world of the sacred, as this sacredness was experienced through a spatial mode of consciousness in which time was perceived to move in eternally recurring seasonal cycles. Yet we now begin to experience the sacred dimension of our new story of the universe as an irreversible emerging process.

No longer are we celebrating simply the seasonal renewal of the living world. We now are experiencing in the world around us the primordial emergence of the universe in the full surge of its creativity. We are integral with the process. We experience the universe with the delight of our postcritical naiveté.

Never before have any people carried out such an intensive meditation on the universe and on the planet Earth as has been carried out in these past few centuries in our Western scientific venture. Indeed, there is a mystical quality in the scientific venture itself. This dedication, this sacred quest for understanding and participation in the mystery of things, is what has brought us into a new revelatory experience. While there is no need for us to be professional scientists, there is an absolute need for us to know the basic story of the universe and of the planet Earth, as these are now available to us by science.

—"The Gaia Hypothesis: Its Religious Implications," in
The Sacred Universe, 115–16

THREE PRINCIPLES: DIFFERENTIATION, SUBJECTIVITY, AND COMMUNION

These governing principles of the universe have controlled the entire evolutionary process from the moment of its explosive origin some fourteen billion years ago to the shaping of the planet Earth, the emergence of life and consciousness, and so through the various ages of human history. These principles, known in past ages by intuitive processes, are now understood by scientific reasoning, although their implications have not yet been acted upon in any effective way. The ecological age must now activate these principles in a universal context if the human venture is to continue. These principles on which the universe functions are three: differentiation, subjectivity, and communion.

Differentiation is the primordial expression of the universe. In the fiery violence of some billions of degrees of heat, the original energy dispersed itself through vast regions of space not as some homogeneous smudge or jellylike substance, but as radiation and as differentiated particles eventually distributed through a certain sequence of elements, manifesting an amazing variety of qualities. These were further shaped into galactic systems composed of highly individuated starry oceans of fire. Everywhere we find this differentiating process taking place. In our own solar system, within the sequence of planets, we find the planet Earth taking shape as the most highly differentiated reality we know about in the entire universe. Life on Earth finds expression in an overwhelming variety of manifestations. So, too, with the human: as soon as we appear, we immediately give to human existence multiple modes of expression. These themselves change through the centuries.

The second primary principle is that of increased subjectivity. From the shaping of the hydrogen atom to the formation of the human brain, interior psychic unity has consistently increased along with a greater complexification of being. This capacity for interiority involves increased unity of function through ever more complex organic structures. Increase in subjectivity is associated with increased complexity of a central nervous system. Then comes the development of a brain. With the nervous system and the brain comes greater freedom of control over the activity of the organism. In this manner planet Earth becomes ever more subject to the free interplay of self-determining forces. With subjectivity is associated the numinous quality that has traditionally been associated with every reality of the universe.

A third principle of the universe is the communion of each reality of the universe with every other reality in the universe. Here our scientific evidence confirms, with a magnificent overview, the ancient awareness that we live in a *universe—a single, if multiform, energy event*. The unity of the entire complex of galactic systems is among the most basic experience of contemporary physics. Although this comprehensive unity of the universe was perceived by indigenous peoples, affirmed by the great civilizations, explained in creation myths the world over, outlined by Plato in his *Timaeus*, and given extensive presentation by Newton in his *Principia*, nowhere was the full genetic relatedness of the universe presented with such clarity as by the scientists of the twentieth century.

—"The Ecological Age," in *The Dream of the Earth*, 44–46

2

Spirituality of Earth

One of the most important contributions of Berry's thought is the sense of the subjectivity of Earth—in each creature and ecosystem as well as in the planet as a whole. This subjectivity provided a context for Berry to speak about the numinous dimension of Earth that evokes awe and wonder. In this he was deeply influenced by the Jesuit scientist, Pierre Teilhard de Chardin (1881–1955).

Teilhard observed that the universe from the beginning had a physical and psychic component—matter and spirit were evolving together over time. From this perspective human consciousness is not an addendum, but rather in continuity with the unfolding universe. While humans manifest a special mode of self-reflective consciousness, we are increasingly aware that other species have their own modes of awareness. The interiority of matter itself, namely, the subjectivity of all things, is that which allows for communion and reciprocity. In addition, this interiority gives rise to patterning and differentiation throughout the universe and Earth. The patterning leads to increasing complexity and consciousness, eventually giving rise to multi-cellular life, fish, birds, animals, and humans. Something in patterning causes it to reach out beyond itself, which has been called emergence. The emergent properties in matter— their self-organizing dynamics—have led to complex life systems.

Berry speaks of this emergence poetically as the "numinous maternal principle out of which life emerges." For this reason, humans are in deep communion with universe and Earth processes. Just as life has emerged from these processes, so human spirituality emerges in relation to the Earth community.

To illustrate how humans placed themselves amidst the spirituality of Earth, Berry draws on the ritual relationships of Native Americans and other indigenous peoples. Humans placed themselves in a world of cosmic powers and an Earth infused with spirituality. They invoked these powers and spirituality to manage the demands of life—rites of passage, inexplicable loss, unmitigated suffering. In a similar manner, the Chinese saw humans as the mind and heart of Heaven and Earth—a self-reflective and affective presence amidst a dynamic living Earth.

This intimacy is what Berry wishes to reawaken—in thanksgiving and reciprocity. These are sensibilities that Berry would discuss with groups on the sun porch at the Riverdale Center. Often he would gesture toward the great red oak just outside the windows of this porch. Noting that this tree was some four hundred years old, he would wonder about its story in the historical setting of Henry Hudson sailing his small ships up the river. He would imagine, as well, the relationship of this bioregion to the geological time of the 200 million-year-old Palisades across the river, and even beyond to universe processes. Berry sensed the kinship and reciprocity with such enduring expressions of life. He felt gratitude for the universe story interwoven with those who gathered under the limbs of the great red oak. Such sensibilities are a counterpoint, he felt, to the devastating losses of life in the Sixth Extinction of species happening today. These are losses, Berry observed, that silence sacred stories.

EARTH SPIRITUALITY

The spirituality of Earth refers to a quality of Earth itself, not a human spirituality with special reference to the planet Earth. Earth is the maternal principle out of which we are born and from which we derive all that we are and all that we have. We come into being in and through Earth. Simply put, we are Earth-lings. Earth is our origin, our nourishment, our educator, our healer, our fulfillment. At its core, even our spirituality is Earth-derived. The human and Earth are totally implicated, each in the other. If there is no spirituality in Earth, then there is no spirituality in us.

Not to recognize the spirit dimension of Earth reveals a radical lack of spiritual perception. . . .

What is needed is a new spiritual, even mystical, communion with Earth, a true aesthetic of Earth, sensitivity to Earth's needs, a valid economy of Earth. We need a way of designating the Earth-human world in its continuity and identity rather than exclusively by its discontinuity and difference. We especially need to recognize the numinous qualities of Earth.

We might begin with some awareness of what it is to be human, the role of consciousness on Earth, and the place of the human species in the universe. While the traditional Western definition of the human as a rational animal situates us among the biological species, it inadequately expresses the role we play in the total Earth process. The Chinese, for example, define the human as the *hsin* of Heaven and Earth. The word *hsin* is written as a pictograph of the human heart. It can be translated by a single word or by a phrase that conveys both feeling and understanding. It could be translated by saying that the human is the "understanding heart of Heaven and Earth." Even more briefly, in this context, we can say that the human is "the heart of the universe." Yet another way to translate *hsin* is to say that we are "the consciousness of the universe" or "the psyche of the universe." Here we have a remarkable feeling for the fullest dimensions of the human, the total integration of reality in the human, and the total integration of the human within the reality of things.

We need a spirituality that emerges out of a reality deeper than ourselves, a spirituality that is as deep as the Earth process itself, a spirituality that is born out of the solar system and even out of the heavens beyond the solar system. For it is in the stars that the primordial elements take shape in both their physical and psychic aspects. Out of these elements the solar system and Earth took shape, and out of Earth, ourselves. . . .

Today we are in a new position where we can appreciate the historical and the cosmic as a single process. This is the vision of Earth-human development that will provide the sustaining dynamic of the contemporary world. We must nourish awareness of this vision. Our language and imagery need to acknowledge both the physical and psychic dimensions of this organizing force. It needs to be named and spoken of in its integral form. Just as we see the unified functioning of particular organisms, so too Earth itself is governed by a unified principle in and through which the total complex of earthly phenomena takes its shape. When we speak of Earth, we are speaking of a numinous maternal principle out of which all life emerges.

—"The Spirituality of the Earth," in
The Sacred Universe, 71, 73–75

THE UNIVERSE MANIFESTS
THE SACRED

The universe is the supreme manifestation of the sacred. This notion is fundamental to establishing a cosmos, an intelligible manner of understanding the universe, or even any part of the universe. That is why the story of the origin of things was experienced as a supremely nourishing principle, as a primordial maternal principle, or as the Great Mother, in the earliest phases of human consciousness. Some of the indigenous peoples of this country experience it as the Corn Mother or as Spider Woman. Those who revere the Corn Mother place an ear of corn with the infant in the cradle to provide for the soothing and security the infant needs to feel deep in its being. From the moment the infant emerges from the warmth and security of the womb into the chill and changing world of life, the ear of corn is a sacred presence, a blessing.

We must remember that it is not only the human world that is held securely in this sacred enfoldment, but the entire planet. We need this security, this presence throughout our lives. The sacred is that which evokes the depths of wonder. We may know some things, but really we know only the shadow of things. We go to the sea at night and stand along the shore. We listen to the urgent roll of the waves reaching ever higher until they reach their limits and can go no farther, then return to an inward peace until the moon calls again for their presence on these shores.

So it is with a fulfilling vision that we may attain—for a brief moment. Then it is gone, only to return again in the deepening awareness of a presence that holds all things together.

—"The World of Wonder," in
The Sacred Universe, 176–77

LIVING IN A UNIVERSE

What do you see? What do you see when you look up at the sky at night at the blazing stars against the midnight heavens? What do you see when the dawn breaks over the eastern horizon? What are your thoughts in the fading days of summer as the birds depart on their southward journey, or in autumn when the leaves turn brown and are blown away? What are your thoughts when you look out over the ocean in the evening? What do you see?

Many earlier peoples saw in these natural phenomena a world beyond ephemeral appearance, an abiding world, a world imaged forth in the wonders of the sun and clouds by day and the stars and planets by night, a world that enfolded the human in some profound manner. This other world was guardian, teacher, healer—the source from which humans were born, nourished, protected, guided, and the destiny to which we returned.

Above all, this world provided the psychic power we humans needed in our moments of crisis. Together with the visible world and the cosmic world, the human world formed a meaningful threefold community of existence. This was most clearly expressed in Confucian thought, where the human was seen as part of a triad with Heaven and Earth. This cosmic world consisted of powers that were dealt with as persons in relationship with the human world. Rituals were established whereby humans could communicate with one another and with the earthly and cosmological powers. Together these formed a single integral community—a universe.

Humans positioned themselves at the center of this universe. Because humans have understood that the universe is centered everywhere, this personal centering could occur anywhere. For example, the native peoples of North America offered the sacred pipe to the powers of the four directions to establish themselves in a sacred space where they entered into a conscious presence with these powers. They would consult the powers for guidance in the hunt, strength in wartime, healing in time of illness, support in decision making. We see this awareness of a relationship between the human and the powers of the universe expressed in other cultures, as well. In India, China, Greece, Egypt, and Rome, pillars were established to delineate a sacred center, which provided a point of reference for human affairs and bound Heaven and Earth together.

There were other rituals whereby human communities validated themselves by seasonal acknowledgement of the various powers of the universe. This is still evident with the Iroquois autumn Thanksgiving ceremony, where the sun, Earth, the winds, the waters, the trees, and the animals each in turn received expressions of personal gratitude for those gifts that made life possible. Clearly, these peoples see something different from what we see.

We have lost our connection to this other deeper reality of things. Consequently, we now find ourselves on a devastated continent where nothing is holy, nothing is sacred. We no longer have a world of inherent value, no world of wonder, no untouched, unspoiled, unused world. We think we have understood everything. But we have not. We have *used* everything. By "developing" the planet, we have been reducing Earth to a new type of barrenness. Scientists are telling us that we are in the midst of the sixth extinction period in Earth's history. No such extinction of living forms has occurred since the extinction of the dinosaurs some sixty-five million years ago.

—"The World of Wonder," in
The Sacred Universe, 170–71

TO WANTONLY DESTROY
A LIVING SPECIES

The ecological age fosters the deep awareness of the sacred presence within each reality of the universe. There is an awe and a reverence due to the stars in the heavens, the sun, and all heavenly bodies; to the seas and the continents; to all living forms of trees and flowers; to the myriad expressions of life in the sea; to the animals of the forests and the birds of the air. To wantonly destroy a living species is to silence forever a divine voice. Our primary need for the various life forms of the planet is a psychic, rather than a physical, need. The ecological age seeks to establish and maintain this subjective identity, this authenticity at the heart of every being. If this is so of the prehuman phase of life, it is surely true of the human also.

—"The Ecological Age," in *The Dream of the Earth*, 46

HUMAN INTIMACY WITH EARTH

Our relationship with Earth involves something more than pragmatic use, academic understanding, or aesthetic appreciation. A truly human intimacy with Earth and with the entire natural world is needed. Our children should be properly introduced to the world in which they live, to the trees and grasses and flowers, to the birds and the insects and the various animals that roam over the land, to the entire range of natural phenomena. . . .

In our own thinking we are coming back to this once more out of our new mode of understanding the universe. We now experience ourselves as the latest arrivals, after some 14 billion years of universe history and after some 4.6 billion years of Earth history. Here we are, born yesterday. We need to present ourselves to the planet as the planet presents itself to us, in an evocatory rather than a dominating relationship. There is need for a great courtesy toward Earth.

This courtesy we might learn from the Haudenosaunee, or Iroquois Indians. Their thanksgiving ritual is one of the most superb ceremonies that humans have ever known. Too long to present in its entirety, it does have a refrain that is relevant here: "We return thanks"—first to our mother, Earth, which sustains us, then on to the rivers and streams, to the herbs, to the corn and beans and squashes, to bushes and trees, to the wind, to the moon and stars, to the sun, and finally to the Great Spirit who directs all things.

To experience the universe with such sensitivity and such gratitude! These are primary experiences of an awakening human consciousness. Such stupendous moments reveal a striking sense of the alluring planet Earth. An intimacy wonderfully expressed in the famous Western Inscription of Chang Tsai, an eleventh-century administrative official in China. This inscription, placed on the west wall of his office, so that he would constantly have it before him, reads quite simply: "Heaven is my father and Earth is my mother and even such a small creature as I finds an intimate place in its midst. That which extends throughout the universe, I regard as my body and that which directs the universe, I regard as my nature. All people are my brothers and sisters and all things are my companions."

Also, Wang Yang-ming, an early sixteenth-century Chinese Neo-Confucian writer, tells us that a truly developed person is someone who realizes that we form one body with Heaven, Earth, and all living things. He mentions "everything from ruler, minister, husband, wife, and friends to mountains, rivers, heavenly and earthly spirits, birds, animals, and plants; all should be truly loved in order to realize my humanity which forms a unity, and then my clear character will be completely manifested and I will really form one body with Heaven, Earth, and the myriad things."

India, too, has an intimacy with the natural world, as expressed in the epic poem *The Ramayana*, with its touching scenes of Rama and Sita in exile, wandering in the forest with its flowering plants, fruit-bearing bushes, elephants, monkeys, deer, and brightly plumed birds. Also in India there are the familiar animal tales of the *Hitopadesa*, the teaching of wisdom through playful narratives of forest life.

Everywhere there is intimacy, the mutual presence of the life community in all its numinous qualities. We, too, have something of this in our own transcendental and romanticist traditions that arose in Germany in the late eighteenth century and came to the English-speaking world through Coleridge in England and Emerson in America. Within this context, we developed our own American feeling for the natural world, expressed in the writings of Walt Whitman, Henry Thoreau, and John Muir. These are the archetypal personalities whose work is continued in writers Aldo Leopold, Loren Eiseley, Mary Austin, Joseph Wood Krutch, Gary Snyder, Edward Abbey, Annie Dillard, Barry Lopez, Terry Tempest Williams, and so many others, and through a multitude of artists and musicians.

With the more recent nature writers a new understanding of the universe begins to take shape. Our scientific understanding of the universe, when recounted as story, takes on the role formerly fulfilled by the mythic stories of creation. Our naturalists are no longer simply romanticists or transcendentalists in their interpretive vision; they have absorbed scientific data into their writings. A new intimacy with the universe has begun within the context of our scientific tradition.

— "Human Presence," in *The Dream of the Earth*, 13–15

3

Rejoining the Earth Community

From Thomas Berry's perspective, our human encounter with the wonder of the natural world complements our inner spiritual journey. Berry understood wonder as an opening into those human spontaneities that he associated with the wild or wilderness. Encounter with the wild was for Berry a way to see into the dynamic dimensions of nature. Rather than looking at nature as an object for manipulation, exploitation, or romantic attachment, Berry saw the soul of humans as resonating with external wilderness. For Berry, authentic human spontaneities are activated by the vastness, as well as intricacy, of the natural world. In these essays, rejoining the Earth community implies coming into renewed relationship with the complex of organic and inorganic beings that make up the ecosystems of each continent.

To do this, one has to expand understanding of how to enter into nature and its porous boundaries. Here Berry urges us to navigate the flow of nature, as we do with human interactions, by drawing on the language of intimacy and distance, of presence and withdrawal. This language of human relations is also helpful for human-Earth relations, as it reveals an understanding of the mutually revelatory character of existence. Each reveals itself to the other and in the revelation something of the mystery of the evolutionary journey is communicated. Those able and willing to see, to sense, and to embrace nature open themselves to a constantly changing and mutually fecund boundary that fosters a spiritual life.

Just as ecologists try to identify the porous edges of different ecosystems, so also Berry realized that different cultural systems and religious traditions border one another so that they can be mutually revelatory and generative. They are differentiated and interrelated in ways that even the historical record tends both to highlight and to mask. For example, the historical record of the world religions brings to light complex interactions and understandings by individuals and communities with the natural world. So also Berry underscores the settling of the North American continent during the era of "manifest destiny" as a masking of the degradation of peoples, animals, plants, soils, and places. He calls us to witness the creative engagement of specific native peoples (such as Pueblo and Dineh-Navajo in the Southwest and Lakota and Crow on the high plains) with the North American continent, even as they bear the burden of centuries of marginalization.

Thus, the spontaneities that arise in the human, by virtue of our being embedded in the swirl of cosmological and ecological stories, are found in every tradition. In this way, Berry acknowledges the emotional charge that the medieval poet Dante achieved in The Divine Comedy. *Such spontaneities burst open when the alienated human heart returns to a center that incorporates the differences within reality. For Berry, this return continues to be particularly challenging in the context of "the unsettling of America." As the noted poet and farmer, Wendell Berry, reminds us in his book of the same title, in our domesticating of the continent, namely, in our active "doing" we have not realized what we have "undone" in terms of ecosystems.*

Berry confronts this violent history of exploited people, land, and species with four questions that serve as spiritual guideposts in his inquiry: How will Euro-Americans move beyond the grip of a rational, exploitative worldview? How can we respond to the devastated native peoples of the continent? How might we recover relationship with animals, in particular their needs for habitat and subsistence? Finally, how will we bear witness to the continent as our way into a viable future?

Berry himself entered many times into dialogue with First Nations leaders, such as at a gathering at Georgian Bay in Ontario, Canada. After hearing Berry speak publicly on this occasion Mohawk leader Tom Porter called him "grandfather." He observed with great emotion that Berry's words reminded him of the elders of his youth. These exchanges and the recognitions they evoked furthered the dialogue of respect for cultural diversity and reverence for ecological integrity.

RETURNING TO
OUR NATIVE PLACE

We are returning to our native place after a long absence, meeting once again with our kin in the Earth community. For too long we have been away somewhere, entranced with our industrial world of wires and wheels, concrete and steel, and our unending highways, where we race back and forth in continual frenzy.

The world of life, of spontaneity, the world of dawn and sunset and glittering stars in the dark night heavens, the world of wind and rain, of meadow flowers and flowing streams, of hickory and oak and maple and spruce and pineland forests, the world of desert sand and prairie grasses, and within all this the eagle and the hawk, the mockingbird and the chickadee, the deer and the wolf and the bear, the coyote, the raccoon, the whale and the seal, and the salmon returning upstream to spawn—all this, the wilderness world recently rediscovered with heightened emotional sensitivity, is an experience not far from that of Dante meeting Beatrice at the end of the *Purgatorio*, where she descends amid a cloud of blossoms. It was a long wait for Dante, so aware of his infidelities, yet struck anew and inwardly "pierced," as when, hardly out of his childhood he had first seen Beatrice. The "ancient flame" was lit again in the depths of his being. In that meeting, Dante is describing not only a personal experience, but the experience of the entire human community at the moment of reconciliation with the divine after the long period of alienation and human wandering away from the true center.

Something of this feeling of intimacy we now experience as we recover our presence within the Earth community. This is something more than working out a viable economy, something more than ecology, more even than Deep Ecology, is able to express. This is a sense of presence, a realization that the Earth community is a wilderness community that will not be bargained with; nor will it simply be studied or examined or made an object of any kind; nor will it be domesticated or trivialized as a setting for vacation indulgence, except under duress and by oppressions, which it cannot escape. When this does take place in an abusive way, a vengeance awaits the human, for when the other living species are violated so extensively, the human itself is imperiled.

If Earth does grow inhospitable toward human presence, it is primarily because we have lost our sense of courtesy toward Earth and its inhabitants, our sense of gratitude, our willingness to recognize the sacred character of habitat, our capacity for the awesome, for the numinous quality of every earthly reality. We have even forgotten our primordial capacity for language at the elementary level of song and dance, wherein we share our existence with the animals, and with all natural phenomena. Witness how the Pueblo Indians of the Rio Grande enter into the eagle dance, the buffalo dance, and the deer dance; how the Navajo become intimate with the larger community through their drypaintings and their chantway ceremonies; how the peoples of the Northwest express their identity through their totem animals; how the Hopi enter into communication with desert rattlesnakes in their ritual dances. This mutual presence finds expression also in poetry and in story form, especially in the trickster stories of the Plains Indians in which Coyote performs his never-ending magic. Such modes of presence to the living world we still carry deep within ourselves, beyond all the suppressions and even the antagonism imposed by our cultural traditions.

Even within our Western traditions at our greater moments of expression, we find this presence, as in Hildegard of Bingen, Francis of Assisi, and even in the diurnal and seasonal liturgies. The dawn and evening liturgies, especially, give expression to the natural phenomena in their numinous qualities. Also, in the bestiaries of the medieval period, we find a special mode of drawing the animal world into the world of human converse. In their symbolisms and especially in the moral qualities associated with the various animals, we find a mutual revelatory experience. These animal stories have playfulness about them, something of a common language, a capacity to care for each other. Yet these movements toward intensive sharing with the natural world were constantly turned aside by a spiritual aversion, even by a sense that humans were inherently cut off from any true sharing of life. At best they were drawn into a human context in some subservient way, often in a derogatory way, as when we projected our own vicious qualities onto such animals as the wolf, the rat, the snake, the worm, and the insects. We seldom entered their wilderness world with true empathy.

The change has begun however, in every phase of human activity, in all our professions and institutions. Greenpeace on the sea and Earth First! on the land are asserting our primary loyalties to the community of Earth. The poetry of Gary Snyder communicates something of the "wild sacred" quality of Earth. In his music Paul Winter is responding to the cry of the wolf and the song of the whale. Roger Tory Peterson has brought us intimately into the world of the birds. Joy Adamson has entered into the world of the lions of Africa; Jane Goodall the social world of the chimpanzees; and Dian Fossey the world of the gorillas. John Lilly has been profoundly absorbed into the consciousness of the dolphin. Farley Mowat and Barry Lopez have come to an intimate understanding of the gray wolf of North America. Others have learned the dance language of the bees and the songs of the crickets.

What is fascinating about these intimate associations with various living forms of Earth is that we are establishing not only an acquaintance with the general life and emotions of the various species but also an intimate rapport, even an affective relationship, with individual animals within their wilderness context. Personal names are given to individual whales. Indeed, individual wild animals are entering into history. This can be observed in the burial of Digit, a gorilla especially close to Dian Fossey. Fossey's own death by human assault gives abundant evidence that if we are often imperiled in the wilderness context of the animals, we are also imperiled in the disturbed conditions of what we generally designate as civilized society.

Just now one of the significant historical roles of the primal people of the world is not simply to sustain their own traditions, but to call the entire civilized world back to a more authentic mode of being. Our only hope is in a renewal of those primordial experiences out of which the shaping of our more sublime human qualities could take place. While our own experiences can never again have the immediacy or the compelling quality that characterized this earlier period, we are experiencing a post-critical naiveté, a type of presence to Earth and all its inhabitants that includes, and also transcends, the scientific understanding that now is available to us from these long years of observation and reflection.

Fortunately, we have in the native peoples of the North American continent what must surely be considered in the immediacy of its experience, in its emotional sensitivities, and in its mode of expressions, one of the most integral traditions of human intimacy with Earth, with the entire range of natural phenomena, and with the many living beings which constitute the life community. Even minimal contact with the native peoples of this continent is often an exhilarating experience in itself, an experience that is heightened rather than diminished by the disintegrating period through which they themselves have passed. In their traditional mystique of Earth, they are emerging as one of our surest guides into a viable future.

Throughout their period of dissolution, when so many tribes have been extinguished, the surviving peoples have manifested what seems to be an indestructible psychic orientation toward the basic structure and functioning of Earth, despite all our efforts to impose on them our own aggressive attitude toward the natural world. In our postcritical naiveté we are now in a period when we become capable once again of experiencing the immediacy of life, the entrancing presence to the natural phenomena about us. It is quite interesting to realize that our scientific story of the universe is giving us a new appreciation for these earlier stories that come down to us through peoples who have continued their existence outside the constraints of our civilizations.

Presently we are returning to the primordial community of the universe, Earth, and all living beings. Each has its own voice, its role, its power over the whole. But, most important, each has its special symbolism. The excitement of life is in the numinous experience wherein we are given to each other in that larger celebration of existence in which all things attain their highest expression, for the universe, by definition, is a single gorgeous celebratory event.

—"Returning to Our Native Place," in
The Dream of the Earth, 1–5

THE NORTH AMERICAN CONTINENT

There is now a single issue before us: survival. Not merely physical survival, but survival in a world of fulfillment, survival in a living world, where the violets bloom in the springtime, where the stars shine down in all their mystery, survival in a world of meaning. All other issues dwindle in significance—whether in law, governance, religion, education, economics, medicine, science, or the arts. These are all in disarray because we told ourselves: We know! We understand! We see! In reality what we see, as did our ancestors on this land, is a continent available for exploitation.

When we first arrived on this continent some four centuries ago, we also saw a land where we could escape the monarchical governments of Europe and their world of royalty and subservience. Here before us was a land of abundance, a land where we could own property to use as we wished. As we became free from being ruled over, we became rulers over everything else. We saw the white pine forests of New England, trees six feet in diameter, as forests ready to be transformed into lumber. We saw meadowland for cultivation and rivers full of countless fish. We saw a continent awaiting exploitation by the chosen people of the world.

When we first arrived as settlers, we saw ourselves as the most religious of peoples, as the most free in our political traditions, the most learned in our universities, the most competent in our technologies, and most prepared to exploit every economic advantage. We saw ourselves as a divine blessing for this continent. In reality, we were a predator people on an innocent continent.

When we think of America's sense of "manifest destiny," we might wish that some sage advice regarding our true role had been given to those Europeans who first arrived on these shores. We might wish that some guidance in becoming a life-enhancing species had been offered during these past four centuries. When we first arrived on the shores of this continent, we had a unique opportunity to adjust ourselves and the entire course of Western civilization to a more integral presence to this continent.

Instead, we followed the advice of the Enlightenment philosophers, who urged the control of nature: Francis Bacon (1561–1626) and René Descartes (1596–1650), who promoted the separation of the conscious self from the world of matter, and John Locke (1632–1704), who saw human labor as the only way to give value to the land. In 1776, when we proclaimed our Declaration of Independence, we took the advice of Adam Smith's (1723–1790) *Inquiry Into the Nature and Causes of the Wealth of Nations*, a book of enormous influence in the world of economics from then until now. Our political independence provided an ideal context for economic dominance over the natural world.

As heirs to the biblical tradition, we believed that the planet belonged to us. We never understood that this continent had its own laws that needed to be obeyed and its own revelatory experience that needed to be understood. We have only recently considered the great community of life here. We still do not feel that we should obey the primordial laws governing this continent, that we should revere every living creature—from the lowliest insect to the great eagle in the sky. We fail to recognize our obligation to bow before the majesty of the mountains and rivers, the forests, the grasslands, the deserts, the coastlands.

The indigenous peoples of this continent tried to teach us the value of the land, but unfortunately we could not understand them, blinded as we were by our dream of manifest destiny. Instead we were scandalized, because they insisted on living simply rather than working industriously. We desired to teach them our ways, never thinking that they could teach us theirs. Although we constantly depended on the peoples living here to guide us in establishing our settlements, we never saw ourselves as entering into a sacred land, a sacred space. We never experienced this land as they did—as a living presence not primarily to be used but to be revered and communed with.

René Descartes taught us that there was no living principle in the singing of the wood thrush or the loping gait of the wolf or the mother bear cuddling her young. There was no living principle in the peregrine falcon as it soared through the vast spaces of the heavens. There was nothing to be communed with, nothing to be revered. The honeybee was only a mechanism that gathered nectar in the flower and transformed it into honey for the sustenance of the hive and the maple tree only a means of delivering sap. In the words of a renowned scientist: "For all our imagination, fecundity, and power, we are no more than communities of bacteria, modular manifestations of the nucleated cell."[1]

In order to counter reductionistic and mechanistic views of the universe such as this, we need to recover our vision, our ability to see. In the opening paragraph of *The Human Phenomenon*,

Pierre Teilhard de Chardin (1881–1955) tells us: "One could say that the whole of life lies in seeing. That is probably why the history of the living world can be reduced to the elaboration of ever more perfect eyes... See or perish. This is the situation imposed on every element of the universe by the mysterious gift of existence."[2] We need to begin to see the whole of this land. To see this continent, we might imagine ourselves in the great central valley that lies between the Appalachian Mountains to the east and the Rocky Mountains to the west. Here we would be amazed at the vast Mississippi River, which flows down through this valley then on into the immense gulf that borders the southern shores of this continent. This massive flow of water, including its tributary the Missouri, flowing in from the northwest, constitutes one of the greatest river systems on the planet, draining almost the entire continent, from New York and the Appalachian Mountains in the east to Montana and the Rocky Mountains in the west.

This region includes the Great Plains, the tall grasslands that extend from Indiana to the Mississippi River, to the short grasslands that begin across the river and extend to the mountains. This is a territory to be honored in some special manner. The region to the west of the river has what are among the deepest and most fertile soils on the planet. Soils that elsewhere are only inches in depth here are several feet deep, soils formed of the debris washed down from the mountains over the long centuries. A large human population depends on this region. Such precious soil is a gift to be carefully tended. This center of commercial wheat, and later corn production, began in New York in the early nineteenth century and extended westward until now it can be located in those Kansas fields of grain that extend beyond the horizon.

When we stand in the Mississippi basin, we can turn westward and experience the mystery, adventure, and promise of this continent; we can turn eastward and feel its history, political dominance, and commercial concerns. Westward are the soaring redwoods, the sequoia, the Douglas fir, the lodgepole pine;

eastward are the oaks, the beech, the sycamore, the maple, the spruce, the tulip poplar, the hemlock. Together, these bear witness to the wonder of the continent and the all-encompassing sea.

We might also go to the desert, or high in the mountains, or to the seashores, where we might really see, perhaps for the first time, the dawn appear in the eastern sky—its first faint purple glow spreading over the horizon, then the slow emergence of the great golden sphere. In the evening, we might see the flaming sunset in the west. We might see the stars come down from the distant heavens and present themselves almost within reach of our arms if we stood on tiptoe.

So too, we might begin to view the change of the seasons: the springtime awakening of the land as the daisies bloom in the meadows and the dogwood tree puts forth its frail white blossoms. We might experience the terrifying moments when summer storms break over the horizon and lightning streaks across the sky, the moments when darkness envelops us in the deep woodlands, or when we experience the world about us as a vast array of powers asserting themselves. When we view all this, we might begin to imagine our way into the future.

Concerning this future we might make two observations. First, the planet Earth is a onetime project. There is no real second chance. Much can be healed because the planet has extensive, albeit limited, powers of recovery. The North American continent will never again be what it once was. The manner in which we have devastated the continent has never before occurred. In prior extinctions, the land itself remained capable of transformations, but these are now much more difficult to effect. Second, we have so intruded ourselves and debilitated the continent in its primordial powers that it can no longer proceed simply on its own. We must be involved in the future of the continent in some comprehensive manner.

It is clear that there will be little development of life here in the future if we do not protect and foster the living forms of this continent. To do this, a change must occur deep in our souls. We need our technologies, but this is beyond technology. Our technologies have betrayed us. This is a numinous venture, a work of the wilderness. We need a transformation such as the conservationist Aldo Leopold (1887–1948) experienced when he saw the dying fire in eyes of a wolf he had shot. From that time on, he began to see the devastation that we were bringing upon this continent. We need to awaken, as did Leopold, to the wilderness itself as a source of a new vitality for its own existence. For it is the wild that is creative. As we are told by Henry David Thoreau (1817–1862), "In Wildness is the preservation of the world."[3] The communion that comes through these experiences of the wild, where we sense something present and daunting, stunning in its beauty, is beyond comprehension in its reality, but it points to the holy, the sacred.

—"The World of Wonder," in
The Sacred Universe, 172–76

4

The Universe as Cosmic Liturgy

Thomas Berry spent many decades living within the rhythms of monastic life. This included liturgical prayers throughout the day—at dawn, at midday, and at dusk. He was embedded in the daily cycles of light and dark. In addition, the monastic community was woven into the great seasonal cycles of birth, death, and rebirth from Christmas to Good Friday to Easter. The liturgical practices of monastic life evoked in him a profound feeling for how humans had traditionally identified themselves with the dynamics of nature and the cosmos, both in religious ceremonies and in daily life. These liturgies and cycles of prayers were ways of orienting and grounding humans amidst the changing rhythms of planetary life and celestial movements.

Berry understood that religious traditions seek to foster symbolic connections of the "Small Self" of the individual and community to the "Great Self" of Earth and the universe. What marks Berry's perspective, however, is not only his appreciation for the symbolic relations of humans to the universe. He also recognized profound changes in modern consciousness due to the theory of evolution. He described the shift in human self-awareness from living in a cosmos in cyclical time to participating in a cosmogenesis, namely, a universe shaped by developmental time. In other words, humans are part of the emergent evolutionary universe and the Earth community of organic and inorganic life.

Berry realized that the ongoing dynamics of the universe, or cosmogenesis, should not be reduced to simply a material and mechanistic process. Rather, cosmogenesis manifests an inherent and inherited "Covenant of the Universe" in which all beings find rapport, validity, and identity. In this context for Berry, all human institutions and occupations are expressions of the universe and the ways in which it functions. In this spirit, Berry expands on Pierre Teilhard de Chardin's spiritual reflections on the allure of scientific research as a form of "covenant" with material reality. Berry recognizes this attraction for research among scientists, from the micro-level of the atom to the macro-level of the galaxies.

The cosmological character of the human is oriented and grounded through liturgy. Religions are noteworthy for their symbol systems that connect human cultures to larger celestial and natural processes, such as star movements, seasons, and the times of the day. For Berry, these "moments of grace," when the sacred clearly communicates itself, both validates and gives identity to cultures and orients them towards a larger rapport with the universe. In these ways the great cosmic liturgies emerged in all the world religions as practitioners communed with the known universe.

By such rituals, Native Americans, for example, bonded a child to their human community, their Earth community of life, as well as the celestial community of stars and planets. So also, the sequence of Chinese dynasties validated themselves, ruled the peoples under their jurisdiction, and created meaning and purpose through cosmic liturgies. In these instances, the political function of these liturgies did not exhaust their fundamental cosmological orientation. Indeed, the relatedness, or mutual rapport, of these liturgies contained generative seeds from which new political orders emerged, as well as explications of death and withering across the varied realms of existence.

In Berry's perspective, the Abrahamic traditions of Judaism, Christianity, and Islam have articulated striking cosmological symbolisms that locate humans largely in the scripture of the word, but also at times in the scriptures of the world. In the modern period, these traditions eventually gave rise to secular and scientific positions. Berry described the alienation and separation from the natural world that resulted from the objectifying studies of the natural sciences. This occurred even as the Western religions consolidated spiritual concerns and ways of knowing almost exclusively in human relations and human-divine concerns. The "dazzling wonder" of the human-Earth and human-cosmic realms was subsumed into symbolisms derived from the scriptures of the word. The irony is that the cosmic liturgies surviving into the present have come out of the complexity of the dynamic universe. However they obfuscate that larger consciousness in spiritualities of the "Small Self," or the individual. Berry sensed that the phenomena, or world of "shining forth," was dimmed from what it had been for earlier peoples.

In this context, his efforts to revisit such an expression of cosmic liturgy as the Omaha peoples' "Introduction of a Child to the Cosmos" appears not as romantic rhetoric. Berry affirms this liturgy as a spiritual ritual locating the stages of human life in the complexities of the living Earth community and cosmological order. Similarly, Berry recognized the thanksgiving prayer of the Haudenosaunee/Iroquois and the magnificent ethnographic testimony of Nicholas Black Elk as different spiritual rituals with similar cosmological orientations. He realized that reducing these moments of grace to only a human experience runs the risk of losing their emphasis on cosmological relatedness across realms of identity and difference. Thus, cosmic liturgies not only invoke the spirits from vastly different realms, but they also reestablish fundamental relationships, such as in the Chinese Confucian world of social harmonies and in the Hindu world of personal cosmic centering. According to Berry, we are challenged to revisit our knowledge of transformative relationships in the cosmos as ways of spiritually orienting ourselves.

THE COVENANT OF THE UNIVERSE

We know more about the universe than any people ever knew. We have more command over the functioning of the Earth than any people ever had. Yet we are less intimate with the universe than peoples of previous times. This can be seen in the work of scientists such as Steven Weinberg, who has written with great insight about the earlier phases of the universe and has remarked that the more we know about the universe the less meaning it seems to have.

When we inquire about just why scientists devote such intense effort, such enduring dedication to research projects concerned with the story of the universe, one answer might be that scientists are answering the irresistible call of the Great Self of the universe to the Small Self of the individual. We are only beginning to be aware that this attraction of the scientist to the study of the universe is itself one of the more fascinating aspects of the universe. Since the universe is the only self-referent mode of being in the phenomenal world, every being in the universe is universe-referent for its origin and destiny and its proper role in the great community of existence. If there is such a thing as human intelligence, then it has emerged out of the universe, and, in its functioning, it must in some manner be ordered toward the universe. The primary study of human intelligence might be designated as universe study or, in a term derived from the Greek, cosmology. Only through understanding the universe can we understand ourselves or our proper role in the great community of existence.

All human occupations and professions must themselves be expressions of the universe and its mode of functioning. This is especially true of what came to be known as religion, for the term *religion* and the term *universe* are somewhat similar in their meaning. Both are derived from the Latin, and both have to do with turning back to unity. Religion, *re-ligare*, is a binding back to origin. Universe, or *universa*, is a turning back of the many to the one. Earlier peoples seem to have understood this. They lived in a pattern of human activities that were validated by their relation with the cosmological sequence. They lived within the Covenant of the Universe, the ontological covenant whereby each component of the universe experienced itself in intimate rapport with the other components of the universe. They constantly evoked their self-consciousness within their universe-consciousness. The one had no meaning without the other.

They situated themselves at each moment in terms of the four cardinal directions governed by their position in relation to the sun. The sun arose in the east, set in the west. At midday the sun was in the south. The north was where the sun never situated itself. The sky was above, planet Earth below. Each person received self-validation by this act of knowing exactly where he was in the universe. So too with any structures erected on Earth. These could only be authentic, even physically secure, by being ordered in relation to the cosmological directions. This required careful alignment with the celestial world whence the sense of direction, as well as the sense of time was derived.

With regard to time and seasons, rituals were established to create a consciousness of the moments of cosmological change: the dawn and dusk of the daily sequence of sunlight and darkness, the increase and decline in the phases of the moon, the winter solstice especially as the danger moment of the universe, the period of dark descent; then came the rise into a world of warmth and light and the blossoming of the plants and the birth moment throughout the mammalian world. These moments of change were the moments when the shining forth of the phenomenal world was most evident. Such moments were moments of grace, moments when the sacred world communicated itself with special clarity to the world of the human.

This intimacy with the universe can be seen in the initiation ceremony of the Omaha Indians. When an infant is born, the child is taken out under the sky and presented to the universe. . . . So too an invocation was made to the powers of the living beings on the planet, and then to the earth and the insects and to all those beings that live within the Earth. In this manner the covenant of Earth was affirmed. Humans asserted their intimacy with Earth and acknowledged their dependence on the larger community for whatever they needed in life.

This was also true in the Chinese world. There, the imperial palace was constructed in such correspondence with the movement of the natural world that the emperor could move from one section of the palace to another with each change of seasons. The colors of the garments worn by the emperor were also coordinated with the changes of the cosmological order. The music was altered to suit the quiet and dark of winter or the brightness and delight of summer. If these correspondences between the human and the cosmological order were not observed, the entire order of the universe would, supposedly, be thrown into disarray.

In Western civilization at an earlier period, the entire structure of Western ritual was cosmologically oriented. This was most obvious in the worship ritual that was extensively coordinated, especially in the Christian monasteries, with the sequence of changes during the day-night cycle. Psalms and hymns were sung in the middle of the night to celebrate the deep contemplative aspect of the nocturnal hours; then came the dawn rituals, the midday and evening rituals. So too at its highest moment of intellectual development the entire theological explanation of Western religion was integrated with physics and metaphysics and cosmology as these were handed down through the Aristotelian tradition. This was the great work of Thomas of Aquinas, to restructure all Christian thought within a cosmological perception. That is why he tells us quite clearly in the prologue to his summary of Christian belief that divine revelation comes to us through two scriptures, the scripture of the natural world and the scripture recorded in the Bible.

—"The Epic of Evolution," in *Evening Thoughts*, 113–16

COSMIC LITURGY

Throughout the premodern period, the universe, experienced as a cosmic liturgy celebrating the grandeur of existence, was the ultimate creative force in the phenomenal order giving shape, resplendence, vigor, and meaning to every mode of being. Above all, it was the primary locus, the primary place for the meeting of the divine and the human. Simply to draw attention to such grandeur of perception and human participation in such ecstatic fulfillment is to awaken a deep wonderment in our modern souls. To us who live in this very secular age, all this appears in a distant world, something of a dream world, a world that we cannot experience as entirely real.

We live too deeply alienated from the cosmological order, the phenomenal world, the world of the "shining forth" (for such is the meaning of the word *phenomena*). We live in a human world, a world where all our values are human. The natural world is experienced as subservient to the human. Its reality has diminished as the human has been magnified. If we give attention to the universe, it is to the scholarly world of scientific equations, of atomic and subatomic particles; to the technological world of mechanistic contrivances; to the economic world of unlimited human use of the Earth as a collection of natural resources.

We seem not to appreciate the dazzling wonder or the sacred dimension that finds expression in the universe itself, a universe that emerged into being by a creativity beyond anything we can imagine, a world that assumed its present form by an unpredictable self-organizing power. What is truly amazing is that these predictable processes, sometimes considered to be random, produced a universe so coherent in its structure and so finely ordered in its functioning amid the turbulence of an awesome and relentless inner creative energy.

Even when we penetrate so deeply into the reality of the physical and the biological orders, even when we understand clearly that the human story and the universe story are a single story, we somehow fail in our ability to tell the story in a way that would provide comprehensive meaning for our human mode of being. In earlier times, a world of meaning was worked out within a universe and a planet moving in ever-renewing seasonal cycles. However, such a world of meaning has not yet been worked out within a universe that has come into being by a primordial flaring forth giving rise to an irreversible sequence of transformation episodes. These episodes move in the larger arc of their sequences, from lesser to greater complexity of structure and functioning and also from lesser to greater consciousness. This unfolding sequence is self-emergent, self-sustaining, self-educating, self-governing, self-healing, and self-fulfilling. From this source must come all emergence, all nourishment, all education, all governance, all healing, all fulfillment.

—"The Epic of Evolution," in
Evening Thoughts, 116–18

THE UNIVERSE AS INTEGRAL TO HUMAN-EARTH RITUALS

Each morning we awaken as the sun rises and light spreads over Earth. We rise and go about our day's work. When evening comes and darkness spreads over Earth, we cease our work and return to the quiet of home. We may linger awhile enjoying the evening with family or friends. Then we drift off into sleep and that dream realm beyond consciousness where our lives are renewed after the exhaustion of the day. As in this day-night sequence, so in seasonal sequences we experience changes in our ways of being. In autumn our children may spend their days in school and we alter our daily regimen accordingly. In springtime we may go out more freely into the warmth of sunshine where some of us plant gardens. In summertime we may visit the seashore to find relief from the limitations that winter imposed upon us. In each of these seasons, we celebrate festivals that give human expression to our sense of meaning in the universe and its sequence of transformations.

Our concern . . . is to offer an overview of the many ways in which the integral dimension of the universe is manifest in different human communities throughout the Earth community. Just now the human community has a remarkable scientific understanding of the universe and of the planet Earth, yet, humans seem not to have the rapport with the universe that earlier humans once hand. Rather than fostering a mutually enhancing relationship with the other members of the Earth community, we have been responsible for causing dysfunction throughout the entire planet. Yet, along with our anthropogenic alterations of Earth's climate, soils, and waters are alternative visions of human-Earth relations, some of which are quite old while others appear dimly on the horizons of our future. Echoes of an ancient human-Earth relationship are evident among indigenous peoples, many of whose sustainable life ways have been significantly altered by contacts with modern industrial cultures.

The ethnography of the Omaha people, formerly living as a tribal group in the northern plains of North America, records a personal relationship with the larger universe that was ritually established at the time of each child's birth. Among this people, a newborn infant was taken out under the sky and presented to the cosmos:

> Ye sun, moon, stars, all ye that move in the heavens,
> I bid you hear me! Into your midst has come a new life.
> Ho! Consent ye, we implore, make its path smooth
> that it may reach the brow of the first hill.
> Ho! Ye winds, clouds, rain,
> All ye that move in the air
> I bid you hear me, into your midst has come a new life.
> Consent ye, we implore, make its path smooth
> that it may reach the brow of the second hill.

The invocation continues to address the hills, rivers, trees and all that lives on Earth with a corresponding request that the child be protected to reach the third hill. The birds that fly in the air, the animals great and small, that dwell in the forests, the insects that move among the grasses—all are invoked. Then a final petition asks that all creatures everywhere will take care of the child that it may travel beyond the four hills. This legacy remains a significant expression of the Omaha sense of the cosmos as liturgical presence.

Assistance from the entire universe is needed if a person is to have both the psychic and the physical powers needed to live through the perils of earthly existence. While invocations like this one are ways of locating the human mode of being within the complex of powers throughout the universe, there are other ways in which the structure of human life and human society is formally coordinated with the movement of the cosmological order through the seasons.

Indeed, the unity of the universe can be observed in the vast array of rituals carried out by diverse indigenous peoples around the planet, as well as by the agricultural and literate societies, especially in their founding stages. The human cultural project in all its phases is authenticated by ritual insertion into the great seasonal sequence whereby Earth is constantly renewed. Thus a calendar of events is established and cosmic rituals are performed at their appropriate times.

Both personal and community affairs are validated by ritual integration of the human venture with the natural world. As with the cycle of the seasons, the periods of transformation in the cosmological order are celebrated by corresponding rituals in the human order. This is evident in the annual thanksgiving celebration of the Haudenosaunee, or Iroquois, confederacy of the St. Lawrence River valley in North America. In their elaborate recitations, these communities honor, through ritual acknowledgements that continue into the present, the beings layered throughout the natural world. For the Haudenosaunee, the human community fulfills its roles in relation to all the various elements that sustain human life. While the winged creatures, four-legged creatures, insects, and all realms of life may be described as "spiritual" in our outsider effort to understand the ritual, what seems more important is that ongoing relationships are established and reaffirmed with these realms of being. Ritual relationships are acknowledged with the rain and the winds, with the mountains, the valleys, the plants, the animals, the homelands, the stars, and the sun in the heavens.

Personal intimacy with cosmic powers also finds expression among other peoples of North America, such as the Siouan-speaking nations, with their sweat-lodge ceremony and vision quest. The initiate, under the guidance of a shamanic personality, spends several days fasting and praying for the strength and orientation needed for future life. At this time the basic symbols that guide and protect a person are awakened in the consciousness of the initiate. A special name may be communicated that relates a person to some guardian life form. A song to be sung at the time of death may be received, a song that will enable the person to pass safely through the perils encountered at this time.

A remarkable example of intimacy with cosmic powers is found in the life story of Nicholas Black Elk, the Lakota/Sioux *wichasha wakan*, or healer. When he was nine years old, he had an astonishing vision relating to his specific historical situation and the destiny of his tribe. Special attention was given to the role of Black Elk himself in guiding the destiny of his people. In his vision, he saw the six grandfathers representing the four directions, the sky, and Earth. At one moment in the prolonged vision, a great stallion in the heavens sang a song that rang out throughout the universe. In the words of Black Elk as narrated to John Neihardt:

> His voice was not loud, but it went all over the universe and filled it. There was nothing that did not hear, and it was more beautiful than anything can be. It was so beautiful that nothing anywhere could keep from dancing. The virgins danced, and all the circled horses. The leaves on the trees, the grasses on the hills and in the valleys, the waters in the creeks and in the rivers and the lakes, the four-legged and the two-legged and the wings of the wind—all danced together to the music of the stallion's song. . . . [1]

As we look back over the course of human affairs, we find among the most significant and universal of human cultural developments is the effort to relate human affairs to the universe through ritual celebrations at certain moments in the annual sequence of the seasons, in the diurnal cycle, as well as in the life cycle of birth, maturity, and death. These events relating human affairs to the ever-recurring events of the natural world provide an authentication of the human mode of being. There is great significance in the coordination of human events, habitation, and communal architecture with the seasonal and astronomical cycles, because such coordination necessitates some awareness of time reckoning, of archaeoastronomy, and of a measured calendar. It led in some societies to precise observation of the phenomena of the sun and moon, the stars, the planets, and the natural phenomena.

In ancient China, the cosmological order and human affairs were seen as existing in profound synchronicities and correlations. These relationships were so close that the entire range of political and social activity of the human world was arranged in accord with seasonal sequences in the natural world. Instructions in the meaning of the rituals are given in the liturgy book known as the *Book of Rites* (*Li Chi*). In this text, the ritual observances for each season are prescribed. One entry gives the following warnings about resulting dilemmas if inappropriate seasonal rituals are performed:

> If in the first month of spring the governmental proceedings proper to summer were carried out, the rain would fall unseasonably, plants and trees would decay prematurely, and the states would be kept in continual fear. If the proceedings proper to autumn were carried out, there would be great pestilence among the people; boisterous winds would work their violence; rain would descend in torrents, mountain spinach, tufted grasses, ryegrass, and southernwood would grow up together. If the proceedings proper to winter were carried out, pools of water would produce destructive effects, snow and frost would prove very injurious, and the first sown seeds would not enter the ground.[2]

The object of all appropriately performed ceremonies is to bring down the spirits from above, and even the ancestors, in order to rectify relations between ruler, ministers, the bioregion, and the larger cosmos. The rituals maintain the generous feeling between father and son, and ensure the harmony between elder and younger brother. They adjust the relations between high and low, and give their proper places to husband and wife. The whole may be said to secure the blessing of Heaven. Humans are seen as the heart and mind of Heaven and Earth, and the visible embodiment of the five elements. They live in the enjoyment of all flavors, the discrimination of all notes, and the engagement with all colors.

In each one of these instances, the integral relationship between the human and the universe was recognized and celebrated within a single community with plural expressions. The relationship was not primarily one of exploitation. The ritual was a bonding of all the diverse components within a single, coherent whole and the purpose of the ritual was the flourishing of the entire range of beings within the universe. The understanding was that the human response was crucial for sustaining an integral functioning of all the diverse relationships throughout the bioregion, the cultural setting, and the larger cosmos.

In some societies, the annual ceremony was a reenactment of the creation of the universe. In Mesopotamia, for example, during a particular historical period, the legend of Marduk and Tiamat was reenacted. Tiamat, the divine embodiment of the waters of chaos, was slain by the warrior deity, Marduk, and in their struggle the structure and diversity of the universe were established. In the Hindu tradition of India, the patterns of ritual relationship of humans and the cosmos are expressed in the *Laws of Manu*. This book embodies ancient oral traditions that came down in several versions from the Vedic period, when the Aryan peoples came into India around 1500 BCE. Eventually the traditions found literate expression in a single text. Here the acceptable pattern of human affairs was given in relation to cosmic order, or *rita*. Along with this, increasingly complex cosmological traditions were expressed in the early writings called the Vedas. The Vedas conclude in wisdom teachings called the *Upanishads* or Vedanta, the "end of the Vedas." Here the individuated self, or *atman*, was integrally linked to the larger universe in the form of the cosmic person, or *Brahman*. On every auspicious communal and individual occasion there was an effort to establish personhood at the center of the universe. The cosmic center, symbolized in script or icon or ritualized sound such as *OM*, is where all things were validated, all things found their meaning and their security.

From this it becomes clear that in antiquity, the primary cultural referent as regards reality, value, and power for religious expression is the universe in all its full plurality and integrity. Every mode of being is universe-referent. Most particularly, with regard to the vast range of created beings that are culturally described and individually experienced, Earth is the immediate basis of cosmological reality and value.

—"The Universe as Cosmic Liturgy," in
The Christian Future and the Fate of Earth, 96–102

CELEBRATING
COSMIC TRANSFORMATIONS

A new cosmological worldview is emerging that provides a new context for liturgy. Presently, our liturgies give magnificent expression to the periods of seasonal renewal and also, at times, to significant historical events or personal achievements. Especially in these moments of renewal, in the springtime of the year, the psychic energies of the human community are renewed in their deepest sources by their participation in the profound changes within the natural world itself.

But now a new sequence of liturgical celebrations is needed. Even more than moments of seasonal renewal, these moments of cosmic transformation must be considered sacred. Only by a proper celebration of these moments can our human spiritual development take place in an integral manner, for these were the decisive moments in the shaping of both our human consciousness and our physical being.

First among these celebrations might be a celebration of the emergent moment of the universe itself. . . . The human mind and all its spiritual capacities began with this moment. As with origin moments generally, it is supremely sacred and carries within it the high destinies of the universe in its intellectual and spiritual capacities, as well as its physical shaping and living expression.

—"The Cosmology of Religions," in
The Sacred Universe, 124

5

Religions Awaken to the Universe

Thomas Berry was primarily a historian of world religions and cultural traditions. He created a remarkable History of Religions program at Fordham University from 1966 to 1979, offering classes ranging from the Western religions and Asian religions to Native American and indigenous religions. Over the course of his years of teaching at Fordham, he developed a profound understanding that the world religions needed to be appreciated not just through their histories, texts, and traditions, but also through their cosmological dimensions.

The History of Religions program at Fordham was new and innovative, especially among Catholic universities. The attraction for students was Berry's approach; he taught these religions as living wisdom traditions, not just as ancient artifacts of culture. This brought the traditions alive for students and ultimately inspired the Harvard conferences on World Religions and Ecology (1996–1998). These were the first conferences to explore views of nature and environmental ethics in the world religions.

As he reflected on the world religions, he would ponder on how they can contribute to our ecological challenges and how they can be related to the great story of the universe. With these realizations, he identified the need for a study of the cosmology of religions, even more than a theological or historical approach. This was (and still is) a major challenge to theologians and scholars of religion. The nature of this challenge for religions, then, is twofold:

1. *to see religions as having cosmological dimensions historically;*
2. *to see religions as responding to the new scientific cosmology being discovered regarding the unfolding of the universe and Earth.*

The first task is to recognize religions as "religious cosmologies," namely, symbolic systems that have provided narratives of where we come from, why we are here, and where we are going. In doing this, they assist humans in seeing themselves as part of a vast universe in which they participate. In all religious traditions, the macrophase of the universe is viewed as resonant with the great self of humans. This is exemplified in the Cosmic Christ of Christianity, the Mahapurusha (great person) in Hinduism, and the Buddha Nature in all reality in Buddhism. Embodying this large self is the goal of spiritual cultivation beyond the limitations and struggles of a personal ego.

As Berry puts it, "The universe is the primary bearer of religious experience; the universe is the larger self of each person." To understand this through the lens of traditional religions is one task of religious scholars, theologians, and lay people. The other is to see this same dynamic connection of humans to the universe through the lens of our understanding of an evolving universe. With the various disciplines of modern science, from astronomy to biology we know we no longer live within a universe that is static.

One of the major discoveries of the last two hundred years is that we live not simply in a cosmos but in cosmogenesis, namely, an evolving universe. This changes everything. Humans are participants in this great journey of the universe because we are born out of this great unfolding. What Berry underscores, drawing on Teilhard de Chardin, is that from the beginning the universe has both a spiritual and physical expression. Thus the very

*structure and form of the universe is revelatory. How we read
this sacred scripture is a major challenge.*

*For as Berry often reminded us, theology departments and
seminaries have missed this in their exclusive concentration on
studies of the written scriptures—the Bible and commentaries, as well as with systematic theology and church history or
homiletics and pastoral counseling. The fact that our ecological destruction is causing the end of a geological era is absent
from the concerns of most theologians and lay people. But Berry
observes in this chapter that, "the human community and the
natural world will go into the future as a single sacred community or not at all." The exploration, then, of both religious cosmology and scientific cosmology provides a way forward for the
future flourishing of the Earth community. New spiritual guides
will be needed for this task.*

THE COSMOLOGY OF RELIGIONS

The universe itself is the primary sacred community. All religious
expression by humans should be considered participation in the
religious aspect of the universe itself. From this perspective we
are moving from the theology and the anthropology of religions
to the cosmology of religions. Throughout the twentieth century
in America, there was an intense interest in the anthropology of
religions, particularly the sociology of religions, the psychology
of religions, the history of religions, and comparative religion.
Because none of these forms of religious consciousness has been
able to deal effectively with the evolutionary story of the universe or with the ecological crisis that is now disturbing Earth's
basic life systems, we are being led to a cosmological dimension of religion both by our efforts at academic understanding
and for practical issues of physical survival on a planet severely
diminished in its life-giving capacities.

What is new about this mode of consciousness is that the universe itself is now experienced as an irreversible time-developmental process, not simply as an eternal, seasonally renewing

universe. We are focused not so much on cosmos as on cosmogenesis. Now our knowledge of the universe comes primarily through our empirical, observational sciences rather than through intuitive or deductive reasoning processes. We are listening to Earth tell its story . . . through the light that comes to us from the stars, through its geological formations, and through the vast amount of data that the biosystems of Earth give us.

In its every aspect, the human is a participatory reality. We are members of the great universe community. We are not on the outside looking in; we are within the universe, awakening to the universe. We participate in its life. We are nourished by this community, instructed by this community, governed by this community, and healed by this community. In and through this community we enter into communion with that numinous mystery whence all things depend for their existence and their activity. If this is true for the entire universe, it is especially true given our human dependence on Earth.

—"The Cosmology of Religions," in
The Sacred Universe, 117–18

NATURAL WORLD AS SCRIPTURE

In this context, we are moving from a theology of religion and an anthropology of religion to a cosmology of religion. This is the direction where, I think, religious studies will inevitably go in the future. In earlier times, our religious inquiry was theological: it was organized around questions concerned with the existence and nature of God and the relation of creatures to God. Later, our religious concerns were largely anthropological, ministerial, and spiritual, organized around such studies as the sociology and psychology of religion and the history of religions. In the immediate future, our religious concerns will, I believe, be more cosmological. They will be more sensitive to the universe as the primary religious mode of being and to ourselves being religious through our participation in the religion of the universe. There will, I believe, be an emphasis on the planet Earth and on the universe itself as a single sacred community.

The natural world will once again become a scriptural text. The story is written not in any verbal text but in the very structure of the universe, in the galaxies of the heavens and in the forms of the Earth. These are phases in the great story that is the primary presentation whereby the ultimate mystery of things reveals itself to us. The sacred community will be recognized as including the entire universe.

The ritual expression of human presence to the divine will include not only the seasonal rituals whereby the human enters into the renewing cosmological order, but also new rituals celebrating those moments of irreversible cosmological transformation that took place in the formation of the galaxies and in the supernova implosions that finally enabled Earth and all those expressions of life and consciousness to come into being on the planet Earth. We will recognize cosmological and biological as well as historical and religious moments of grace.

More can be said here in dealing with this subject of religion and the academic study of religion in the Ecozoic era. They can at least be hinted at by saying that a new phase of religious studies may be developing, one aimed at overcoming our human and religious alienation from our larger, more comprehensive, sacred community of the natural world. This new discipline has a certain urgency, because if this alienation is not overcome, our other studies may, in the not too distant future, become irrelevant. Of one thing we may be sure: the human community and the natural world will go into the future as a single sacred community or we will both experience disaster.

This, then, is our challenge—to move from a purely human-oriented or personal-salvation focus in our religious concerns to one that embraces the universe in all its forms. This will require an immense shift in orientation, one that recognizes our emergence out of the long evolution of the universe and of Earth. The study of religion will begin to reflect this orientation in the cosmology of religion.

—"Religion in the Ecozoic Era," in *The Sacred Universe*, 99–100

THE CHALLENGE TO THEOLOGIANS

From observable scientific evidence, we understand the story of the universe as an emergent process with a fourfold sequence: the galactic story, the Earth story, the life story, and the human story. Together these constitute for us the primordial sacred story of the universe.

The original flaring forth of the universe carried the present within its fantastic energies just as the present expresses those primordial energies in their articulated form. This includes all of the aesthetic, psychic, and spiritual developments that have occurred across the centuries. The universe, in its sequence of transformations, carries within itself the comprehensive meaning of the phenomenal world. In recent secular times, this meaning was perceived only in its physical expression. Now we perceive that universe has been a spiritual and a physical reality from the beginning. This sacred dimension is especially evident in those mysterious moments of transformation the universe has passed through during its fourteen billion years of existence. These are moments of great spiritual and physical significance: the privileged moments in the Great Story. The numinous mystery of the universe now reveals itself in a developmental mode of expression, a mode never before available to human consciousness through observational processes.

Yet this seems not to mean much to our contemporary theologians. They remain concerned with scriptural interpretation, spiritual disciplines, ministerial skills, liturgy, the history of Christianity, the psychology of religion, and religious pedagogy. None of these areas of study has a direct concern for the natural world as the primary source of religious consciousness. This is one of the basic reasons why both the physical and spiritual survival of Earth has become imperiled. Presently, we in the West think of ourselves as passing into another historical period, in a continuation of the long series of historical transformations that have taken place in the past and that are continuing on into the future. This perception is understandable. If we think, however, that the changes taking place in our times are simply another moment in the series of transformations that passes from classical-Mediterranean times through the medieval era to the industrial and modern periods, then we are missing the real magnitude of the changes taking place. We are, in fact, at the end of a religious-civilizational period. By virtue of our new knowledge, we are changing our most basic relations to the world about us. These changes are of a unique order of magnitude.

Our new acquaintance with the universe as an irreversible developmental process can be considered the most significant religious, spiritual, and scientific event since the emergence of the more complex civilizations some five thousand years ago. At the same time, we are bringing about a devastation of Earth such as the planet has never experienced in the four and a half billion years of its formation.

We are changing the chemistry of the planet, we are disturbing the biosystems, and we are altering the geological structure and functioning of the planet, all of which took some hundreds of millions and even billions of years to bring into being. This process of closing down the life systems of the planet is making Earth a wasteland, and we hardly realize that with each species of life on Earth we lose we also lose modes of divine presence, the very basis of our religious experience.

Because we are unable to enter into the new mystique of the emergent universe, we are unable to prevent the disintegration of the life systems of the planet taking place through the misuse of that same scientific vision. Western religions and theologies have not yet addressed these issues nor established their identity in this context. Nor have other religious traditions been any more successful. Mainstream religions have simply restated their belief and their spiritual disciplines in a kind of fundamentalist pattern.

We cannot resolve the difficulties we face in this new situation by setting aside the scientific venture that has been in process over these past two centuries, especially during this twenty-first century. It will not go away. Nor can we assume an attitude of indifference toward this new context of earthly existence. It is too powerful in its total effects. We must find a way of interpreting the evolutionary process itself. If interpreted properly, the scientific venture could even be one of the most significant spiritual disciplines of these times. This task is particularly urgent, since our new mode of understanding is so powerful in its consequences for the very structure of the planet Earth. We must respond to its deepest spiritual content or else submit to the devastation that is before us.

I do not consider that fundamentalist assertions of our former traditions can themselves bring these forces under control. We are not engaged simply in academic inquiry. We are involved in the future of the planet in its geological functioning and biological survival, as well as in the future of our human and spiritual well-being. We will bring about a physical and spiritual well-being of the entire planet or there will be neither physical nor spiritual well-being for any of our earthly forms of being.

The traditional religions have not dealt effectively with these issues nor with our modern cosmological experience because they did not originate in nor were they designed for such a universe. Traditional religions have been shaped within a dominant spatial mode of consciousness, that is, a mode of consciousness that experiences time as a renewing sequence of seasonal transformations. Although Judaism, Christianity, and Islam have a historical-developmental perspective in dealing with the human process, they lack an awareness of the development of the universe itself. They seem to have as much difficulty as any other tradition in incorporating an understanding of the developmental character of the universe.

Although antagonism toward an evolutionary universe has significantly diminished in Christian theology, our limitations as theologians in speaking the language of this new cosmology is everywhere evident. If much has been done in process theology in terms of our conceptions of the divine and the relations of the divine to the phenomenal world, this has been done generally in the realm of systematic theology. Little has been done in the empirical study of the cosmos itself as religious expression.

—"The Cosmology of Religions," in
The Sacred Universe, 118–21

UNIVERSE AS PRIMARY BEARER
OF RELIGIOUS EXPERIENCE

To envisage the universe in its religious dimension requires that we speak of the religious aspect of the original flaring forth of the universe, the religious role of the elements, and the religious functioning of Earth and all its components. Since the human in its religious capacities emerges out of this cosmological process, then the universe itself can be considered the primary bearer of the religious experience. As Thomas Aquinas (1225–1274) tells us: "The order of the universe is the ultimate and noblest perfection in things."[1] Although Aquinas was thinking of the universe in terms of its renewing seasonal sequence and not as an emergent sequence of irreversible transformations, the same principle applies. The universe is the primary referent in all human understanding.

This way of thinking about the emergent universe provides a context for the future development of the world's religious traditions. Indeed, the peoples of the world, insofar as they are being educated in a modern context, are now able to identify themselves in time and space in terms of the universe as this is presently described by our modern sciences. The problem is that they are not learning the more profound spiritual and religious meaning also indicated by this new sense of the universe.

This story of the universe is at once scientific, mythic, and mystical. Most elaborate in its scientific statement, it is among the simplest of creation stories. Most of all it is the story that we learn from the universe itself. We are finally overcoming our isolation from the universe and beginning to listen to the universe's story. If until recently we were insensitive in relation to its more spiritual communication, this is no longer entirely true. In this understanding, we have an additional context for understanding all the religious traditions, just as our more recent cosmologies do not negate but add to the Newtonian worldview and enable us to deal with questions that could not be dealt with in the Newtonian context. Now we have additional depth of spiritual understanding through our listening to the universe in ways that were not available through our traditional insights. Just as we can no longer live simply within the physical universe of Newton, we can no longer live spiritually in any adequate manner simply within the limits of our earlier religious traditions.

—"The Cosmology of Religions," in
The Sacred Universe, 121–22

PARTICIPATING IN THE JOURNEY OF THE UNIVERSE

The first contribution this new perspective on the universe makes to religious consciousness is the sense of participating in the creation process itself. We bear within us the impress of every transformation through which the universe and the planet Earth have passed. The elements out of which Earth and all its living beings are composed were shaped by supernovae. We passed through the period of stardust dispersion resulting from this implosion-explosion of a first-generation star. We were integral with the attractive forces that brought those particles together in the original shaping of Earth. We felt the gathering of the components of the earthly community and experienced the self-organizing spontaneities within the megamolecules, out of which came the earliest manifestations of the life process and the transition to cellular and organic living forms. These same forces that brought forth the genetic codings of all the various species were guiding the movement of life toward its expression in human consciousness.

This journey, the sacred journey of the universe, is the personal journey of each individual. We cannot but marvel at this amazing sequence of transformations. No other creation story is more fantastic in its account of how things came to be in the beginning, how they came to be as they are, and how each of us received the special characteristics that give us our personal identity. Our reflexive consciousness, which enables us to appreciate and to celebrate this story, is the supreme achievement of our present period of history. The universe is the larger self of each person, since the entire sequence of events that has transpired since the beginning of the universe was required to establish each of us in the precise structure of our own being and in the larger context in which we function.

—"The Cosmology of Religions," in
The Sacred Universe, 122–23

n

A DEGRADED OUTER WORLD
LEADS TO A DEGRADED INNER WORLD

Right now, the human is a devastating presence on the planet. While ostensibly humans are acting for their own benefit, in reality they are ruining the conditions for their own survival and well-being. This applies to both our physical and spiritual survival, since the inner world of the soul needs to be activated by experience of the outer world in all its grandeur.

The pathos of the present is that the human community has lost its capacity to interact creatively with the other components of the planet Earth. This includes the landscape of the planet; the nurturing qualities of the air, the water, and the soil; the energy flow that enables the dynamic powers of Earth to continue their functioning; the life systems that are integrated in an immense complex of patterns beyond full human understanding.

While human beings have never had a comprehensive understanding of the mysteries manifest in the world about them, in former times they had, through their religious traditions, a capacity for being a creative presence within the ever-renewing sequence of life upon Earth. In the closing years of the twentieth century and the dawn of the twenty-first, we seem to have lost this capacity. Instead, because of our population growth and technological power, we have become a deleterious presence throughout the planet. We thought that we were improving the human situation; in reality we were devastating human life along with all the other components of the Earth community. Just now we have begun to realize what we have done.

We realize that a degraded outer world leads immediately to a degraded inner world.

A recovery of the sublime meaning of the universe could lead both to a greater intimacy of the human with the manifestation of the divine in the natural world and to a greater intimacy of the different religions among themselves. It becomes increasingly clear that humans have a common origin and a common destiny with every other component of the Earth community. We live on the same planet. We breathe the same air. We drink the same water. We share the same sunlight. We are nourished by the same soil. In all these ways we share a common spiritual mode of being and a common physical sustenance.

—"Religion in the Twenty-First Century,
in *The Sacred Universe*, 80–81

RELIGION ARISES FROM
WONDER AND AWE

Religion, we must remember, is born out of the sense of wonder and awe of the majesty and fearsomeness of the universe itself. The great decline of religion in industrialized countries can be attributed in large part to the loss of an experience of the grandeur of the natural world, because of our newly acquired technological control over so many aspects of the natural world. At present, we are completely encompassed by the world of human artifice.

This alienation from the natural world deprives us of the immediacy and intimacy with the natural world that we observe in indigenous peoples the world over. In their immediacy with the natural wonders of the world about them, these peoples have an intimate relationship to the sacred as manifest throughout the planet. The world is attractive yet threatening, benign yet fearsome. Divine powers enable fruits, berries, nuts, and vegetation to come forth. These same powers bring the monsoon rains and the withering desert winds, the arctic chill, temperate warmth, and tropical heat.

These experiences evoke in the human soul a sense of mystery and admiration, veneration and worship. This is beyond what is sometimes thought of as nature worship. Recognition of the divine as manifested in nature can be found in the teachings of all the spiritual traditions of the world—even in the teaching of Saint Paul in the first chapter of his epistle to the Romans (v. 20).

Humans feel a need to integrate with these forces in order to survive and to fulfill their human roles in the order of things. Ever present in the human soul is a certain anxiety due to the limited understanding of humans and the fragility of human powers. There is a consciousness that if we fail in the fulfillment of our obligations in the order of the universe, then Earth will not provide the necessities that enable life to survive in any integral manner.

The very purpose of our religious rituals is to enable us to enter into the dramatic manifestation of the divine in a sacred world. This is why we have bodies capable of movement and sensation and minds with a capacity for ritual. Through our sacred ceremonies, we enter into the primordial liturgy of the universe itself.

—"Religion in the Twenty-First Century," in
The Sacred Universe, 82–83

COMMUNION OF SUBJECTS

In the emerging Ecozoic era, we experience the universe as a communion of subjects, not as a collection of objects. We hear the voices of all the living creatures. We recognize, understand, and respond to the voices of the crickets in the fields, the flowers in the meadows, the trees in the woodlands, and the birds all about us; all these voices resound within us in a universal chorus of delight in existence. In their work on *Biophilia*, E. O. Wilson and Stephen Kellert have emphasized the feeling of humans with the larger array of living beings.

We in industrial America are beginning to recognize that the human is a subsystem of Earth systems and that our first obligation in any phase of our human lives is to preserve the integral functioning of the larger world on which we depend. We were brought into being in and through Earth. We survive through our intimate presence to Earth. While this is true in economics, governance, and the healing sciences, it is also true in religious affairs, since we are members of a single sacred community that includes every component of earthly reality.

—"Religion in the Twenty-First Century,"
in *The Sacred Universe*, 86

RENEWING EARTH: FROM ANTHROPOCENTRISM TO ECOCENTRISM

The task of renewing Earth belongs to Earth, as the renewal of any organism takes place from within. Yet we humans have our own special role, a leading role in the renewal, just as we had the dominant role in the devastation. We can fulfill this role, however, only if we move our basic life orientation from a dominant anthropocentrism to a dominant ecocentrism. In effecting this change we need to listen to the voices of Earth and its multitude of living and non-living modes of expression.

We should be listening to the stars in the heavens and the sun and the moon, to the mountains and the plains, to the forests and rivers and seas that surround us, to the meadows and the flowering grasses, to the songbirds and the insects and to their music especially in the evening and the early hours of the night. We need to experience, to feel, and to see these myriad creatures all caught up in the celebration of life.

—"Women Religious," in
The Christian Future and the Fate of Earth, 73

EXTINCTION IS FOREVER

We especially need to hear the creatures of Earth before it is too late, before their voices are stilled forever through extinctions occurring at such a rapid rate. Once gone they will never be heard again. Extinction is forever. The divine experience

they communicate will never again be available to humans.
A dimension of the human soul will never be activated as
it might have been. None of the wonders of the human can
replace what we are losing. However, to speak of the voices
of the natural world is to become suspect to some "religious"
people, for the Western religious traditions have developed
a suspicion of such attitudes toward nature, devaluing them
as simply "pagan" or "animistic" notions. We have lost sight
of the fact that these myriad creatures are revelations of the
divine and inspirations to our spiritual life.

—"Women Religious," in
The Christian Future and the Fate of Earth, 73–74

WONDER, BEAUTY, INTIMACY

Our inner spiritual world cannot be activated without experience of the outer world of wonder for the mind, beauty for
the imagination, and intimacy for the emotions. If we lived on
the moon, our minds would be limited in their development,
our imagination would be as empty as the moon; our emotions
would be as dull. Our sense of the divine would reflect the desolation of the lunar landscape.

—"Women Religious," in
The Christian Future and the Fate of Earth, 74

THE UNIVERSE IS A SINGLE
MULTIFORM CELEBRATORY EVENT

Through our contact with the natural world we learn that the
universe throughout its vast extent in space and throughout its
long sequence of transformations in time is a single multiform
celebratory event. Our role is to enter into this celebration in a
special mode of conscious self-awareness, for this celebration
is the divine liturgy, the purpose of all existence, a celebration
begun in time but continued through eternity.

To save the integrity of this celebration is the first lesson in
survival, for this is the context of all the productivity of the

planet, as well as our primary experience of the divine. If we fail to enter into this celebration, if we seek simply to exploit the myriad creatures about us, then they will fail to produce their fruits and the grand cycle of existence will be diminished. This indeed is already happening.

We, and our children, are becoming unresponsive to the natural world. We live in a world of computers, cell phones, digital photography, television, highways and automobiles, supermarkets, and trivial plastic playthings for our children—all fostered by inescapable advertising aimed at stirring our deepest compulsions to buy and consume. Our education is focused on producing skills associated with the production, distribution, and use of such a multitude of objects with none of the exaltation of soul provided by our experience of natural phenomena. We no longer realize that the universe is a communion of subjects, not a collection of objects—subjects to be communed with as divine manifestation, not objects to be exploited solely for economic gain.

—"Women Religious," in
The Christian Future and the Fate of Earth, 74–75

A FUNCTIONAL COSMOLOGY FOR EDUCATION AND RELIGION

Among the controlling professions in America, the educational and the religious professions should be especially sensitive in discerning what is happening to the planet and the value of these symbols in restoring a certain integrity to the human process. These professions present themselves as guiding our sense of reality and value at its ultimate level of significance. They provide our life interpretation. Education and religion, especially, should awaken in the young an awareness of the world in which they live, how it functions, how the human fits into the larger community of life, the role that the human fulfills in the great story of the universe, and the historical sequence of developments that have shaped our physical and cultural landscape. Along with this awareness of the past and present, education and religion should communicate some guidance concerning the future.

The pathos of these times, however, is precisely the impasse that we witness in our educational and religious programs. Both are living in a past that is fundamentalist or venturing into New Age programs that are often trivial in their consequences, unable to support or to guide the transformation that is needed in its proper order of magnitude. We must recognize that the only effective program available as our primary guide toward a viable human mode of being is the program offered by Earth itself.

Both education and religion need to ground themselves within the story of the universe as we now know it through our empirical ways of knowing. Within this functional cosmology we can overcome our alienation and begin the renewal of life on a sustainable basis. The story is a numinous revelatory story that could evoke not only the vision but also the energies needed for bringing ourselves and the entire planet into a new order of survival.

—"The Viable Human," in *The Great Work*, 70–71

INVOCATION NOT DOMINATION

Religion rectifies not by domination but by invocation. This is the attitude and the power needed. Indeed, our difficulties have been caused principally by a certain distrust of Earth and by a managerial mania seeking to replace or manipulate the marvelous variety and interlacing of the interior life forces of nature with mechanistic processes and chemical concoctions ultimately ruinous to the entire biosphere, the great web of life encircled by Earth. A new appreciation of and confidence in Earth is needed, along with a capacity for communion with it. Only through this comprehensiveness can we really have community. Only through an *integral community* can we survive.

—"The Third Meditation," in
The Christian Future and the Fate of Earth, 12

ECOLOGICAL SPIRITUALITY
AND THE INTEGRAL ECOLOGIST

During the contemporary period, the spiritual and intellectual guides of our Western tradition have shown themselves to be inadequate to their task, however adequate they may have been in former times. A new type of spiritual guide is needed. Previously, Benedictine monks established themselves as the guides for our Western endeavor, by cultivating the soil through physical labor and by copying and explaining the great literary works of the past through their intellectual effort. Later in the medieval period, when the cities of Europe were reestablished, it was the new spirituality of the cathedral builders, university professors, and mendicant friars who guided the course of human affairs. In the medieval period came the political, social, and economic establishments that brought about a sense of national identity and later a sense of the people as competent to determine their own destiny.

Toward the end of the nineteenth century, a new set of guides appeared: research scientists, technologists, engineers, and above all corporate leaders. These persons were determined, through technological exploitation of the planet and its resources, to lead humans into a new golden age. The corporations, supported by the dominant political forces, were determined to seize power over every aspect of the planet. This effort at control has led to our present impasse in human-Earth relations. In particular, it has led to the radical disruption of the major life systems of the planet.

Throughout this modern period, the traditional spiritual leaders—scholars, religious teachers, and social reformers—have been unable to provide sufficient guidance. They have failed to recognize that the basic issue is not simply divine-human or inter-human relations but human-Earth relations and, beyond that, relations with the comprehensive community of the entire universe, the ultimate sacred community. This failure has led to the plundering of the planet by good persons, even deeply religious persons, for the supposed temporal and spiritual benefit of the human. This plundering of the planet to serve human purposes is what needs to change. The industrial movement, with its ideal of subjection of the planet, must now give way to the ecological movement. Only such an ideal will sustain the integral functioning of both the human and nonhuman components of the planet in a single integral community.

This ideal requires a new spirituality. We need the guidance of the prophet, the priest, the saint, the yogi, the Buddhist monk, the Chinese sage, the Greek philosopher, and the modern scientist. Each of these personalities and their teaching are immensely important in their own proper field of functioning. Yet, for these times they might all be considered limited as guides to the human process in its rapport with the natural life systems of the planet. We now have a new understanding of the universe, how it came into being and the sequence of transformations through which it has passed. This new story of the universe is now needed as our sacred story. Few of the traditional spiritual guides seem able to accept this understanding as a revelatory experience. This can only be done by an ecologically sensitive personality.

We need an ecological spirituality with an integral ecologist as spiritual guide. While we can expect this to be realized in only a partial and inadequate manner in any individual, we can still assert that such a spiritual personality is needed. We can also say that the spiritual ideal of former ages was realized in an unlimited variety of individual personalities and rarely in a manner sufficiently striking to become a referent for imitation by others. So too will the ecologist serve as a guide for these times. The great spiritual mission of the present is to renew all the traditional religious-spiritual traditions in the context of the integral functioning of the biosystems of the planet. This is what the project that began at Harvard at the Center for the Study of World Religions has undertaken. With a series of ten conferences, books, and a website, over eight hundred religious scholars, scientists, and activists have examined the resources of the world's religious traditions to meet the spiritual and ethical challenge of the environmental crisis. Ten volumes have been published, a journal, *Worldviews*, has been established, a Forum on Religion and Ecology is now located at Yale.[2]

Until recently, there has been a feeling in most religious traditions that spiritual persons were not concerned with any detailed understanding of the biological order of Earth. Often, the spiritual person was in some manner abstracted from concern with the physical order of reality in favor of the interior life of the soul. If attention was given to the physical order, this was generally in the service of the inner world. This neglect of attention to the natural world permitted those concerned with the more material things of life to take possession of the planet's land and wealth. It permitted the exploitation of the natural world for human gain. The integral ecologist can now be considered a normative guide for our times. The integral ecologist would understand the numinous aspect of a universe emergent from the beginning. The sequence of transformative moments of the universe would be understood as cosmological moments of grace to be celebrated religiously with special rituals. But above all, these moments would appear as revelatory of the ultimate mystery of the universe itself.

The integral ecologist is the spokesperson for the planet in both its numinous and its physical meaning, just as the prophet was the spokesperson for the deity, the yogi for the interior spirit, the saint for the Christian faith. In the integral ecologist, our scientific understanding of the universe becomes a wisdom tradition. We will finally appreciate that our new understanding of a universe that comes into being through a sequence of irreversible transformations has a revelatory dimension. This fresh understanding of the universe establishes a horizon under which all the traditions will henceforth need to function in their integral mode of self-understanding.

—"An Ecologically Sensitive Spirituality," in
The Sacred Universe, 134–37

THE GREAT WORK OF
THE WORLD RELIGIONS

New religious sensitivities emerge as we understand better the story of the universe, which is now available to us through scientific inquiry into the structure of the universe and the sequence of transformations that have brought the universe, the planet Earth, and all its living creatures into being. This new scientific story of the universe has a mythic, narrative dimension that lifts this story out of a prosaic study of data to a holistic spiritual vision.

This new creation narrative enables us to enter into the deep mystery of creation with a new depth of understanding. It is our human version of the story that is told by every leaf on every tree, by the wind that blows across the fields in the evening, by the butterfly in its journey south to its winter habitat, by the mountains and rivers of all the continents of Earth.

Through this story we understand with new insight how every component of the universe is integral with every other member of the universe community. To be is to contribute something so precious that nothing before or afterward will ever contribute that special glory to the created world. Through this story we learn something about how the primordial mystery of the universe brought the planet Earth into being as the most blessed of all the planets we know of. We learn how life emerged and took on such an immense variety in its forms of expression. We learn too how we were brought into being and guided safely through the turbulent centuries. In our contemplation of how tragic moments of disintegration over the course of the centuries were followed by immensely creative moments of renewal, we receive our great hope for the future. To initiate and guide this next creative moment of the story of Earth is the Great Work of the religions of the world as we move on into the future.

—"Religion in the Twenty-First Century,"
in *The Sacred Universe*, 86–87

6

Intercommunion of World Religions

One of the great contributions of Thomas Berry to the study of religions is his understanding that we need the world religions to face our multiple challenges. While he recognized the limitations of religions in their institutional forms, he read the texts and traditions with perspicacity and insight for our present moment. He drew forth the depth components of the world religions for fresh spiritual energies for persons, society, and nature. He wrote widely on the cultivation of virtue, and the strengthening of community, and on care for the natural world. His profound reading of the spiritual dynamics of the world religions is evident in his essay on the Confucian virtues—how they are cultivated and how they contribute to the formation of an authentic human person. In terms of society, he developed a balanced assessment of the emphasis on the individual in the West and on the community in China. He recognized virtues, such as filial piety and humaneness, as both personal and cosmic. As one cultivated these qualities in oneself, one was expressing filiality and love to Heaven as Father and Earth as Mother metaphorically but also biologically.

Berry's study of the world religions over many decades made him one of the first to recommend not just dialogue among religions but intercommunion. This was more than according respect or celebrating diversity among religions (which he certainly did), but it involved an in-depth study of the languages, texts, and history of the traditions. He accumulated a vast library of world religions, some ten thousand books, including primary texts in their original language and commentaries, as well as histories of these traditions.

Hence he was not simply doing a theology of world religions through the lens of Christianity, nor was he doing a comparative study of the traditions. Rather, he was calling forth the wellsprings of wisdom for transformation and intercommunion. This was more than interreligious dialogue, as valuable as this has been. It moved beyond comparing views of God or views of salvation. His perspective reached out into a form of intercommunion of the highest level of appreciation and affection. He viewed these traditions as indispensable contributions of the human family—richly differentiated and yet unified in the call of the human for meaning, purpose, and direction amidst sorrow, loss, and suffering. His empathy for the great struggles embedded in human life empowered him to bring into the modern West these fonts of wisdom bearing insight and compassion.

Thomas's studies of these traditions and commentaries on them remain luminous through the decades. His journey to China in 1948–49 was more than a trip for personal interest. It was to begin to retrieve the wisdom in the traditions of Asia to illuminate our present path. He did that in his book on Buddhism *and in his book on* Religions of India. *Although he didn't complete a book on the religions of China, he wrote several essays on the Confucian tradition, which was a primary source of inspiration for him. It is in writing about this tradition that he made one of his most enduring contributions.*

SPIRITUAL TRADITIONS AND
THE HUMAN COMMUNITY

In antiquity nothing was undertaken in the human order by humans alone. It had to be done in alliance with both cosmic and spiritual processes. Any integral activity involved a three-fold aspect: human, spiritual, and natural. This triple aspect was especially true in human affairs. No effective functioning was considered possible except in alliance with a broader area of reality. . . .

There are presently four main religious issues facing the human community in its spiritual aspect. The first is the grounding of the various spiritual traditions; the second is the activation of the macrophase of each tradition; the third is the intercommunion of the traditions, and the fourth is the entry of the traditions into alliance with the newly developed cosmological myth of modern science. . . .

The deepest energies of all human traditions are needed to deal with contemporary challenges. The most profound human disciplines are needed, for the final decisions in economics and politics as well as in military and diplomatic affairs are ultimately made, not by technology or computers, but by humans subject to both visionary hopes and moods of desperation. But most of all at the present time there is a need to work with sustained human energies through periods of great darkness.

—"Spiritual Traditions and the Human Community," in
The Christian Future and the Fate of Earth, 2–4, 6

GLOBAL MEETING OF THE WORLD RELIGIONS

All human traditions are dimensions of each other. If, as Christians, we assert the Christian dimension of the entire world, we must not refuse to be a dimension of the Hindu world, of the Buddhist world, of the Islamic world. Upon this intercommunion on a planetary scale depends the future development of the human community. This is the creative task of our times, to foster the global meeting of the nations and of the world's spiritual traditions.

—"Spiritual Traditions and the Human Community," in
The Christian Future and the Fate of Earth, 5

RICHNESS OF DIVERSITY

Diversity is enrichment. For the biblical concept of deity to be the universal concept to the elimination of *Shiva* and *Vishnu*

(Hinduism), of *Kuan-yin* and *Amida* (Buddhism), of *Shang-ti* and *T'ien* (Confucianism), of *Orenda*, *Wakan-tanka* and the *Manitou* (Native American), would be to impoverish the concept of the deity. To consider the Christian Bible to be the only scripture, to the elimination of the Vedic hymns, the *Upanishads*, and the *Bhagavad Gita* of India; to the elimination of the *Qu'ran* of Islam, the *Lotus Sutra* of Buddhism, the sacred Books of China, would be to constrict rather than to expand our understanding of divine-human communication.

For any situation the ideal is the greatest tension that the situation can bear creatively. Although every archetypal model needs multiple realizations, the sacred, more than any other element of reality, needs variety in its modes of expression. The difficulties experienced by Christians in accepting the variety of religious traditions can be resolved:

1. By distinguishing between the microphase membership and macrophase influence of all religious traditions
2. By identifying the unique communication of Christian revelation in both modes of its expression (the natural world and scripture)
3. By recognizing the qualitative differences in religions and fostering these differences
4. By identifying the creative dynamics of inter-religious relations
5. By fostering a sense of the new story of the universe as context for understanding the diversity and unity of religions. . . .

I suggest this context for interpretation of the diversity, identity, and inter-communication of religions. It might be considered as a cosmological-historical approach over against the traditional theological, sociological, or psychological approaches to the subject. This cosmological approach accords with the basic statement of Saint Thomas concerning the cosmic community as the "perfection of the universe," as the supreme reality, which "participates in the divine goodness more perfectly, and represents it better than any single creature whatsoever." It also accords with the view of Pierre Teilhard de Chardin (1881–1955) that "[The human] is a *cosmic* phenomenon, not *primarily* an aesthetic, moral, or religious one."[1]

> —"The Catholic Church and the Religions of the World," in
> *The Christian Future and the Fate of Earth*, 22–24

MULTIFORM GLOBAL RELIGIOUS TRADITIONS

What can be seen . . . is that, after the weakening of spiritual and cultural consensus in recent times, the former isolated situation [of religions] can hardly be reestablished. The various religious traditions are irrevocably altered in their individual and collective significance. Our entire spiritual situation—the very mode of our religious consciousness—is changed. Suggestions that the sources of revelation be broadened for Christian theology, that multicultural and multireligious hermeneutics be now a central question, that the Christian tradition be studied according to the norms of the history of religions, that comprehensive study be given to divine revelation, and that a world scriptural collection be developed—these might be among the most significant issues to occupy our efforts in the immediate future. These will shift the content of Western Christian awareness into a new context, the multiform global religious traditions of humankind.

If, formerly, Christianity was studied from the inside out, it should be now studied from the outside in. In this situation, historians of religions are among the foremost religious creators of the twentieth century, primarily responsible for evoking consciousness of a universal human religious heritage in all its diversity. Also, they are responsible for creating the conditions in which extensive interaction of religious traditions and cultures is begun, to be continued indefinitely into the future. Of all the forces at work in the modern world, it is doubtful if any is more powerful than an enlightened religion in awakening ancient traditions to new phases of development. For none of the traditions are in themselves complete. Seeming for long periods to remain unchanged, these traditions are now awakened to development and renewal as seldom before in their history. They begin to realize that they are not entirely stable forms of life but rather developmental processes that have changed considerably in the past and are destined, perhaps, for even greater change in the future.

Yet since these traditions have all undergone extensive interaction with other traditions over the past several thousand years, we should not exaggerate the newness of modifications brought about in the present. The sense of novelty results only from a more heightened intercommunion of traditions due to the definitive nature of present-day intercommunion, its comprehensiveness, and its pervasive nature, all results of modern means of communication. These means are bringing peoples and traditions of the world into one another's presence to a degree never before possible.

Strangely enough, the very forces moving various cultures and religions out of the traditional into the modern world are exactly the forces enabling each tradition to recover contact with its most pristine forms and ancient literatures. Thus these traditions live more deeply in the past even as they move into the present and future. Each tradition is made more complete within itself, more integral with its primordial moments. From this earliest period, the historical movement of religions and cultures has been converging toward multiform global expression in which each finds its place and each is in some manner present to the entire human society.

—"Religion in the Global Human Community,"
in *The Sacred Universe*, 33–34

RELIGIONS OF INDIA AS PART OF THE LEGACY OF HUMANKIND

Hinduism, Yoga, and Buddhism are no longer merely Indian traditions, they are world traditions. . . . Now they are part of the universal human heritage; even the creative aspect of these traditions is no longer an exclusive concern of India. Humanity is now an integral part of the Indian spiritual process. What happens to these traditions in the future will be as much a product of forces outside of India as of forces within India. Already an extensive influence is felt on Hinduism from without the country. To a corresponding degree the Indian religions are affecting the religious-spiritual thought and emotions of humankind. Study of these traditions is a part of these traditions. We as Westerners have ourselves entered into the Indian religious process by the very fact of our study and our effort at understanding these traditions and giving expression to them within the context of our present. Thus the Indian traditions are occupying the world even as the other world traditions are now occupying India. The Indian traditions are now a part of our own intellectual and spiritual life as we become a part of its historical development. We can no longer live adequately without the Indian spiritual traditions, nor can these traditions do without us.

There is an urgency in our understanding these traditions, for we are involved in the spiritual shaping of the world universal, not simply in the study of this world. This shaping of a world in the present requires continuity with the past. We are determined by these traditions even while we are determining these traditions. The past itself is an aspect of the present. For the first time we are bringing the world spiritual traditions into a common human heritage. This is not only a study; it is a creative spiritual process. Those studying the world religions are themselves creating this common spiritual heritage. One of the great tasks to which our age is called is that of giving spiritual shape and substance to the world society now in the process of formation. This new vision of the past is a creation of the present with infinite consequences for the future.

In every phase of life, in the intellectual, artistic, and spiritual aspects of life, the total human past is now the past of each people and each individual person. We do not live only in the West or even primarily in the West; we live in the world, the total world of humans. The achievements of India and China are now available to us and form part of our own heritage, as do the cultures of Japan and Persia and Africa. This is the period of the worldwide expansion of the mind in all areas of life. The global spiritual past is the only adequate context for present understanding of humans even though this effort at universal awareness is thwarted by exclusivist attitudes that still exist in the world. Even now, however, the futility of such exclusivism is widely recognized. All live currents of thought seek to encompass the full dimensions of humankind.

Within this larger world of humankind, the multiple spiritual and humanist traditions implicate each other, complete each other, and evoke from each other higher developments of which each is capable. These traditions implicate each other, for each has a universal mission to humankind. Each is panhuman in its significance. None can be fully itself without the others. Each has a distinctive contribution to make to human development that can only be made by itself. Each must therefore be kept distinctive even as it reaches a universal diffusion among humans. For any tradition to withhold itself from the other societies of humankind or for any to exclude the other traditions is to vitiate and stultify its own tradition and development, to condemn itself to sterile isolation from the only forces that can give it life and creativity. All human traditions are dimensions of each other.

—"The Creative Present,"
in *Religions of India*, 193–94

CONFUCIAN VIRTUES: PERSONAL, SOCIAL, AND COSMIC

But here [we can] identify one of the principal aspects of the Confucian view of those virtues whereby individual capacities are activated in both their microphase and macrophase expression. Those virtues generally recognized as goodness, righteousness, decorum, and understanding constitute what might be considered the personal discipline whereby the full range of personal, social, and cosmic relations is carried out. Yet there is also a series of what might be called the *meta* or comprehensive virtues with a primary concern for the macrophase or cosmic dimensions of the individual. These may be listed as humaneness (*ren*), authenticity (*cheng*), reverence (*jing*), and filial piety (*xiao*). These four have a special status.

Humaneness is a particular virtue and also a comprehensive virtue. As a primary and comprehensive virtue it can be presented as identical with Heaven itself: "The highest humanity rests with Heaven for Heaven is humaneness itself."[2] Because Heaven (*tian*) in some sense is *ren*, then *ren* is normative for all existence. In this comprehensive role, *ren* enables a person to regard "Heaven and Earth and all things as one body. There is nothing that is not part of his self."[3] A further clarification of this statement of the unity of the microphase and macrophase of the individual person involves this statement of Cheng Yi that if one does not activate this virtue in his own being "he will be thousands of miles away from Heaven and Earth and the myriad things."[4]

Cheng, translated as "authenticity," has a remarkable presentation in the *Doctrine of the Mean*. It is the virtue that reaches deep within the *Urgrund* of personal existence to an ultimate power capable of transforming the human community and the entire universe. This power is correlative with the heavenly and natural powers and, with these, originates, sustains, and transforms the universe itself.

Jing, meaning "reverence," is the special virtue manifested by Yu at the very origins of Chinese civilization. It radiates a sense of sacred awe with which the individual regards the universe in its lowest and most particular, as well as in its highest and most universal aspects. This virtue of reverence was considered so ultimate in its origin that it was a prerequisite for later development not only of the particular virtues but even of that most powerful meta-virtue of authenticity. It is indicated by Cheng Yi that those who have not yet attained the virtue of authenticity must first establish in themselves this interior state of reverence. There is such richness in this term, and it is used in such varied nuances, that it is difficult to enunciate the more basic significance out of which the multiple meanings emerge. It seems to involve an attitude of awe at the mystery of things, even at the mystery of one's own being, that predisposes a person toward that modesty of deportment that enables particularity to integrate itself at the most profound level of human feeling with the universality of things. This disposition enables a mutual indwelling to take place between the particular individual and the magnificent and myriad world without. Through this virtue, Yu disposed himself for his spatial presence to Heaven above and Earth below and to the four extreme points of the world. Then he proceeded to integrate human affairs temporally with the sequence of the seasons. His constant reiteration, especially to the ministers, was "Be reverent, be reverent!"[5]

Filial piety (*xiao*) is that special virtue associated with origins. Origin moments are sacred moments, for these give to beings their very existence. This capacity to stand forth magically out of a prior nonexistence into existence is always related to another existence. To this prior existence a unique and absolute reverence is due. This virtue is a metaphysical and ontological as well as a moral mode of being. Without filiality there would be nothing. The phenomenal universe exists in itself and in all its relations only by the power of this virtue. The *Classic of Filial Piety (Xiaojing)* says that filial piety "is the first principle of Heaven, the ultimate standard of Earth, the norm of conduct of the people."[6] The power of this encomium to filial piety was felt not only by the Chinese but also by the Japanese, especially by the Neo-Confucian Nakae Toju in the seventeenth century: "Filial piety is the root of humans. When it is lost, then one's life becomes like a rootless plant . . . What brings life to Heaven, life to Earth, life to humans and life to all things, is filial piety."[7] Elsewhere he envisages filial piety as something like the world soul of Plato: "Filial piety dwells in the universe as the spirit dwells in humans. It has neither beginning nor end; without it is no time or any being; there is nothing in all the universe unendowed with filial piety."[8]

From all of this we can see that in China interrelatedness is grounded not in any religious covenant, nor in any social contract, but in the very origin, structure, and functioning of the universe. To think that human society comes together by some "contract" would be as foolish as to think that the sun and the moon or the wind and the waters established formal contracts with each other in some negotiated way.

—"Individualism and Holism in Chinese Traditions:
The Religious Cultural Context,"
in *Confucian Spirituality*, vol. 1, 46–48

HUMANENESS

Confucian thought gave the clearest expression to the intimacy of beings with one another in its splendid concept of *ren*, a word that requires translation according to context by a long list of terms in English: humaneness, love, goodness, human-heartedness, affection. All beings are held together in *ren*, as in the epistle by St. Paul (1 Colossians 1:17), where he notes that "all things are held together in Christ." Another perhaps even better analogy is in Newton's universal law of gravity, whereby each particle of matter attracts and is attracted to every other particle in the universe. The law of gravity indicates a mere physical force of attraction, whereas the universal law of attraction for the Confucians is a form of feeling identity.

For this reason, in Confucianism, there is the universal law of compassion. As the early Confucian thinker Mencius (372–289 BCE) suggested, this is especially observable in humankind, for every human has a heart "that cannot bear to witness the suffering of others." When the objection was made to the Neo-Confucian Wang Yang-ming (1472–1529) that this law of compassion is evident only in human relations, Wang replied by noting that even the frightened cry of the bird, or the crushing of a plant, or the shattering of a tile, or the senseless breaking of a stone immediately and spontaneously caused pain in the human heart. This would not be, he tells us, unless there existed a bond of intimacy and even identity between ourselves and these other beings.

Recovery of this capacity for subjective communion with Earth is a consequence and a cause of a newly emerging spirituality. Subjective communion with Earth, identification with the cosmic-Earth-human process, provides the context in which we now make our spiritual journey. This journey is no longer only the journey of Dante (1265–1321) through the heavenly spheres. It is no longer simply the journey of the Christian community through history to the heavenly Jerusalem. It is the journey of primordial matter through its marvelous sequence of transformations, in the stars, in Earth, in living beings, and in human consciousness. This journey is an ever more complete spiritual-physical intercommunion of the parts with one another, with the whole, and with that numinous presence that has manifested throughout this entire cosmic-Earth-human process.

—"The Spirituality of the Earth,"
in *The Sacred Universe*, 78–79

WESTERN INDIVIDUALISM AND CHINESE HOLISM

The Western emphasis on excess rather than containment, on adversary relations, on the titanic conflict with deity as expressed in the Promethean story, on the principle of Heraclitus that "war is the father of all things," on the Christ-Anti-Christ conflict in the redemptive process, on the Faustian dissatisfaction with any achieved state, on the social Darwinist "survival of the fittest"—all this has given to the West its aggressive and destructive qualities, but also much of its creativity. The Western world has been restless, has found difficulty in accepting limits, has been merciless in its own self-criticism, as well as oppressive in its demands on others. Western history may be seen as a series of assaults against the limitations of the human condition. This has given to the West its tradition-destructive, society-destructive, and nature-destructive aspects. Much of this is associated with an extreme commitment to individualism. Yet there exist vast creative aspects of this process. The West lives marginally to the human in the hope of expanding the human by exceeding all existing boundaries, while the Chinese lived [in their traditional cultures] centrally in the human seeking to activate those vast creative instincts that emerge from the fathomless depths of the Great Tao.

The main instruments of Western assault in recent centuries has been science as combined with technology. These have given to Western society an experience of the universe and a corresponding capacity to interact with the deepest forces of the universe such as could never have been attained except through the violent assault on all limits and all restraining obstacles to human inquiry into the nature and functioning of the world. The presuppositions of this inquiry have been creativity of conflict, the need for assault against the sacred, the primacy of analysis over synthesis, nonconformity as a basic requirement for personal growth, and ultimately nonconformity for the intellectual and cultural development of society. This is driven by a feeling that every possibility must be tried in searching toward a more expansive vision and experience of the universe. In this context we perceive the reversal of values. Reverence and irreverence change places—so too order and chaos, wisdom and folly, creativity and destruction, the primacy of the society and the primacy of the community.

It is an awesome and astounding adventure. This is a turbulent process always present, if somewhat controlled, in earlier Western development, but in more recent times it is shaken loose from its former limitations to suddenly bring about undreamed-of changes in the entire human-Earth situation. We still have no adequate assessment of these changes in terms of their ultimate creativity and destructiveness, yet the present period reveals itself as one of entrancement with quantitative modes of knowing, with mechanistic rather than organic processes, and with exploitive relations with the natural world. These exploitive relations concern not only the natural world but also the human world.

This exploitation began with the Western drive toward expansion in all its economic, political, social and cultural dimensions of the last five hundred years. By the nineteenth and twentieth centuries the technologies of the West were sufficiently developed that neither the natural world nor human societies could adequately limit Western expansion. It is important, however, to understand the multivalent aspects of this tide of Western influence, especially in relation to individualism. Ironically, this expansionist thought around the world was often considered by Westerners as the liberation of other peoples from the confinements of cultural determinations and from conformity to tribal custom or cultural fixations. Traditional harmonies needed to be shattered; the traditional sense of the sacred needed to be abandoned. The value structure was to be changed. Briefly stated, the organic metaphor of reality, of society, and of the individual was to be replaced by a more atomistic sense of reality and a more legalistic metaphor of social relations based to a large extent on the ultimate value of the individual.

While China tried consistently throughout the nineteenth century to contain itself and its ancient ideals rooted in the integrity of its traditions, it found at the end of the century that it would need to enter a new period of turmoil. China would need to enter developmental history and to modify its dominant organic-person metaphor by the journey metaphor of the Western world.

The Chinese had possibly developed their doctrine of individuality as far as it could be developed within the context of this basic organic metaphor, which might be considered primarily a spatial metaphor. The tree symbolism referred to in the beginning of the *Great Learning* is a very significant symbol in Chinese tradition. This tree grows within a universal space. The individual in the macrophase of one's being experiences a certain radiant presence throughout this space and a certain biological and geological identity with all those beings, those ten thousand beings, that live and move and have their being in this space.

For the Western world the basic symbolism is more temporal than spatial. Journey, historical journey, requires movement, change, and transformation on a scale not compatible with established rituals or with fixed patterns. Yet it must be recognized here that we are speaking not of the journey through seasonal time or of a journey toward a fixed center in space, such as the journey to the center in a mandala context. Nor are we speaking of the journey of Ulysses back to his prior home, or even of the journey of Rama, the journey into exile and return. We are speaking here of the more comprehensive journey of the emergent universe, a unique and irreversible journey of galactic systems, of Earth formation, of living forms, of human community—a journey passing through a sequence of unpredictable discontinuities more extensive than is generally thought possible or even desirable in a more traditional context. In the West these transformations have been considered necessarily beneficial. The West in the past few centuries has been driven by a mythic sense of inevitable progress. This sense of progress and of journey originated in the biblical journey, especially in the exodus from Egypt to Palestine. It was historically interpreted further by Daniel, by John the Evangelist, by St. Augustine, and by Joachim of Flores as primarily a spiritual sequence of developments within a fixed universe. Later, in the period of Frances Bacon and in the eighteenth-century French Enlightenment, the journey was experienced as "progress," especially as progress of human understanding as in the ten stages of human intellectual development outlined by Condorcet; then as the journey of social improvement in the nineteenth-century by Fourier, St. Simon, and Marx; as metaphysical journey by Hegel; as biological journey by Darwin; and finally as the immense journey of the universe by physicists and cosmologists of the twentieth-century. This journey in recent times has been seen as activated by and terminating in individuals with a willingness to deviate from existing norms, even the most sacred norms of belief and of action.

The biological and even the geological structure and functioning of the planet were no longer normative as in the ancient ritual Books of the Chinese. These as well as social bonds were seen as restrictive unless subordinated to human exploitive processes whereby the great journey was now being carried forward. The planet itself, swept up in a vortex of change, was being consumed for human individual advantage.

By the mid-twentieth century, the ancient dialectic observed by the Chinese in the Great Tao had begun to assert itself. After intensive activity, quiet; after four centuries of particularity, wholeness; after a period of temporal discontinuity, a spatial expansion and continuity; after individualism, holism. So now the West experiences with a certain admiration the Chinese expression of relatedness, wholeness, inner cultivation, spontaneity, authenticity, universal reverence, communion with all the living and nonliving components of the universe community.

These tendencies manifest themselves even from within the Western process itself. This we observe in the attraction of the West toward the organicism of Whitehead, toward the biological integrity of the planet presented by Lewis Thomas, toward the hologram metaphor of David Bohm, the synchronicity of Carl Jung, the integral dynamics of the post-industrial solar village of John and Nancy Todd, toward a sustainable economy grounded in the living cycle of renewable resources, and eventually toward a functional cosmology wherein the human personality experiences itself in both its microphase and macrophase of the universe itself. Now we can move toward understanding a macrophase that has both traditional spatial and historical temporal dimensions. Such a macrophase activates the society—individual relations in a greater tension than is generally the case, on the principle that the most desirable state of an organism is not in its highest degree of harmony, but in the greatest tension between order and chaos that the organism can bear creatively. This includes a modified doctrine of individualism.

But if the West appears destined to express itself in a modified form of individualism, China, it seems, is destined to express itself in a modified form of its doctrine of humanity. China has not only a cosmos to commune with but a journey to take. So far, China has kept in a single functional vision what in the West has been divided: the primordial integrity of the universe, the existential order of historical time, and the future order of harmonious presence of the heavenly, the earthly, and the human to each other. In China these three are overlays on each other. The Age of Yu and Shun is simultaneously primordial, present, and future; it is a memory to be kept, an ideal to guide the present, and a future to work toward.

History in the West originated in dividing these three stages in clear and definitive terms. So, too, with the individual and the society, the West differentiates these and places them in an extreme tension with each other. We might almost say that the West is activated more by fission processes while China is activated by fusion processes. As both fission and fusion in the nuclear world produce extraordinary energies, so those vast energies for sustaining and developing the great civilizations can be produced by either process. While such an analogy should not be mentioned in anything more than a passing and suggestive way, it does indicate in some slight manner the differences that can be taken in human affairs with special reference to the interaction between the individual and the society.

In some manner also, these different approaches imply their opposites. The extensive commitment to tension and conflict in the West implies an extraordinary confidence in the capacity of the social structure to sustain this tension without disintegrating. So too the commitment to community on the part of the Chinese goes with an understanding that the support of the total community, and even of the entire natural world, is necessary to sustain the full development and expression of the individual. We might conclude by observing that, while these patterns of society—individual interactions will possibly remain identifying features of Chinese and Western traditions, these traditions may in the future find it helpful to take greater cognizance of each other.

—"Individualism and Holism in Chinese Traditions:
The Religious Cultural Context,"
in *Confucian Spirituality*, vol. 1, 50–54

LOVE AS A COSMIC FORCE

What is remarkable throughout the Asian world is that terms designating supremely affectionate qualities carry ultimate cosmological significance. So in the Chinese world, *ren*, a term translated as love, benevolence, or affection, is not only an emotional-moral term, it is also a cosmic force. This can be said also of the virtue of *ch'eng*, translated as sincerity or integrity. In India, the term *bhakti*, devotional love, was a cosmological as well as spiritual force. In Buddhist tradition, the term *karuna*, compassion, is a supreme cosmic power. Thus we find a pervasive intimacy and compassionate quality in the very structure of the universe and of Earth itself.

Our own quest for a more intimate and benevolent human presence to Earth in our times might reflect these precedents. But even more, perhaps, we might consider our intimate compassionate presence to Earth as originating ultimately in the curvature of space, as it is presented in modern science. The entire Earth community is enfolded in this compassionate curve whereby the universe bends inwardly in a manner sufficiently closed to hold all things together and yet remains sufficiently open so that compassion does not confine, but fosters, the creative process.

This curve that finds its first expression in the physical bonding of the universe and later in the living process of Earth finds its most intimate expression in human thought and affection, as well as in our art, music, and dance. We can hear anew *The Creation* of Hayden and the *Ode to Joy* of Beethoven. We can read anew *Leaves of Grass* by Walt Whitman. We can understand the great intuitions the ancients had of the universe. We can dance anew to the rhythms of Earth.

This reenchantment with Earth as a living reality is the condition for our rescue of Earth from the impending destruction that we are imposing upon it. To carry this out effectively, we must now, in a sense, reinvent the human as a species within the community of life species. Our sense of reality and of value must consciously shift from an anthropocentric to a biocentric norm of reference.

—"Human Presence,"
in *The Dream of the Earth*, 20–21

7

The Challenge to Christianity

Thomas Berry was raised in a large Catholic family in North Carolina. Three of his sisters entered religious life and he remained a priest in the Passionist Order throughout his life. His commitment to Christianity is clear, yet his wide reading on ecological issues led him to ponder why Christians were not responding. This was of immense concern to him and he spoke widely to religious orders of nuns and other Christian groups about environmental issues. He hoped that Christianity, as well as the other religions, would awaken to the critical nature of what was happening to the planet.

Berry recognized that, since the rise of agriculture, all human civilizations have impacted their regions of the globe. However, the spread of industrial economies are now all-pervasive in their deleterious effects. The Promethean drive to manipulate matter and better the human condition are closely related to Western religious and salvific aspirations. Underlying the spread of global industrialization to other regions of the globe were forces with pseudo-spiritual dimensions such as technical efficiency, a work ethos that set aside cultural values, and a desire for cheap labor and products. These ideological drives, presented as a hope for economic progress, masked the reality that this globalizing worldview was devouring the planet.

Yet, Berry also saw that simply fixating on the immensity of the challenges can be enervating. Instead, he searched for spiritual motivations that would not only address the changes required, but would also evoke in Christianity those revelatory sensitivities needed to enhance human relationships with Earth. For example, among Christians, the Cosmic Christ of the universe as expressed by John's Gospel and Paul's Epistles signifies a unifying dimension of the sacredness of the universe. From out of this arises the realization that humans form a single community with the living Earth.

Christians in the industrial era, however, have grown accustomed to seeing the world as simply natural resources for our economic exploitation. Now, for Berry, the challenge is not only to open to the plurality of religious views of the universe, but as well to the story that science presents of an evolving, emerging universe in which humans are embedded. Paradoxically, this opening is also an innovative engagement with detachment. For Christians detachment recalls ascetic practices often dismissed in our secular age such as setting limits on consumption and needs. For Berry, this presents a challenging meditation on the relationships of the wisdom of the cross and the wisdom of the world, namely, sacrifice and withdrawal from the world versus engagement and affirmation of the world.

Over its history, but most particularly in recent centuries, Christianity has been shaped by religious, philosophical, and economic forces that situate the world as background to human drama or as a distraction to spiritual achievement. Thus, detachment has typically led to rejection of the material world as meaningful for spiritual realization. The future Christian challenge, on which may hang the fate of Earth, is recognition of the redemptive wisdom of the cross that complements the Christian belief in Christ's incarnation as the embodiment of the sacred. Accepting this challenge means not opposing the cross and the world, or seeing the cross as symbolic of redemption from out of fallen nature. The spiritual vision Berry proposes integrates the cross and cosmology, social justice and ecojustice. The suffering of Christ and the suffering of planet Earth are one.

In this view, environmental justice aspires to create peace among humans through a complementary ecojustice that acknowledges peace with Earth. The injustices and evils of our economic system are not understood as bounded by oppression of humans alone. Rather, social injustice is located within a larger frame of the diminishment of life itself. For example, whenever we diminish difference, wherever it is found, we diminish the sacred. Religious detachment derives from our fundamental need to transcend our condition and emerge through wonder into the sacred. The need for ascetic withdrawal calls us to a paradoxical affirmation of traditional wisdom even as we move toward new cosmological and ecological understandings. If in the past we sought to save ourselves by detaching from the world, we realize that now we cannot save ourselves without preserving the world in which we live.

The detachment of Christians from the sacred in Earth is particularly poignant when they abdicate responsibility for conserving Earth's ecosystems, leaving this primarily to secular environmental organizations. Berry observes how there have not been adequate voices in the Christian or other religious communities articulating the connections of the sacred to the world. Now, however, Christians are called to a new commitment. What has changed is the challenge of a new story, namely, a narrative of the emergent universe out of which we arise and in which we are embedded. This challenge differs from earlier technological revolutions, such as the invention of the radio in the early twentieth century and our massive reliance on computers in the twenty-first century. The magnitude of our contemporary situation confronts humans at a basic level of knowing. We are challenged to know what the world has been saying to us all along.

We have had inklings of this in our liturgies celebrating seasonal transformations. We have linked these seasonal and celestial transformations to our great religious revelations, but now the cosmological understanding of our world strikes to the heart of our knowledge of wisdom. In the early Christian period, a Trinitarian wisdom derived from Greek philosophy identified

106 THOMAS BERRY

the integral nature of creation, redemption, and inspiration. Berry brings this faith experience into the ecological context by articulating the Trinitarian oneness of Father as principle of differentiation, Son as Word of inner articulation, and Spirit as bonding force in which the universe coheres.

For Berry, the sacred cannot be separated from deep encounters with meaning inherent in the emergence of the universe. The ultimate mystery of reality charges through all the religious languages of God, Great Spirit, and the pervasive presences in the world about us. This love that embraces us in the curvature of space has brought us to self-conscious human reflection. Acknowledging this reality may not eliminate our feeling of estrangement from nature, but it may transform our sense of separation within the great community of life.

THE CHRISTIAN FUTURE
AND THE FATE OF EARTH

The Christian future, in my view, will depend above all on the ability of Christians to assume their responsibility for the fate of Earth. The present disruption of all the basic life systems of Earth has come about within a culture that emerged from a biblical-Christian matrix. It did not arise out of the Buddhist world or the Hindu or Chinese or Japanese worlds or the Islamic world. It emerged from within our Western Christian-derived civilization. If these other civilizations were not ideal in their presence to the natural world . . . their intrusion, in its nature and in its order of magnitude, nowhere approaches the disturbance brought about by our modern Western disruption of the planetary process.

Although our Western industrial civilization was itself a deviation from Christian ideals, it came originally from within a Christian context. In its historical expression it could not have arisen out of any other tradition. We might conclude then that the Christian tradition is susceptible to being transformed in this direction. Until we accept the fact that our central beliefs carry with them a vulnerable aspect we will never overcome our present failure to deal with the increasing disruption of the planet. If the planet fails then we fail, not only as Christians but even as humans. . . .

That Christians are ill-adapted to deal with these issues is clear from their general lack of concern for what is happening. Christians are somewhere off in the distance as, indeed, are most of the professions and institutions of our society. Probably in this country there is more understanding of the problem and there are more effective efforts at its solution outside the churches than within the churches. . . .

. . . Stewardship does not recognize that nature has a prior stewardship over us as surely as we have a stewardship over nature, however different the implications of these modes of stewardship. It does not enable us to overcome our lack of responsiveness at its deepest level. If we hear the voices of the natural world, these are not the fraternal voices heard by Saint Francis of Assisi but the voices of subservient creatures. . . .

. . . In my view, the first step in achieving any adequate human or Christian activity in saving the planet from further irreversible dissolution is to recognize that the universe story, the Earth story, the life story, and the human story—all are a single story. Even though the story can be told in a diversity of ways, its continuity is indisputable. . . .

. . . I propose that new religious sensitivities need to be developed. In former times if such a situation had existed, a new religion might have arisen. But the time is over, apparently, when a religion like any of the classical religions could come into being. What is needed now is not exactly a new religion but new religious sensitivities in relation to planet Earth that would arise in all our religious traditions. The model for these new sensitivities might well be the sensitivities that can be observed in the earlier, more primordial religions, sensitivities that can still be found among some of the tribal peoples of the world.

While these traditions are sometimes considered nature religions possessing none of the grandeur or authenticity of the Christian religion with its transcendent monotheistic personal deity-creator of a world clearly distinct from himself, still they contain insights into the basic relations of humans to the natural world that we are desperately in need of just now and that we cannot articulate within the context of our own resources. The most needed of these insights is the realization that humans form a single community with all the other living beings that exist upon Earth.

In accord with the teachings of Saint Paul and Saint John we might perceive that there is a Christ dimension to this more extensive community of Earth and that what we do to this community we do in some manner to Christ himself. It is difficult to believe that God created such a beautiful world if it were not also the divine intention to redeem, sanctify, and bestow eternal blessing upon it throughout eternity.

—"The Christian Future and the Fate of Earth," in
The Christian Future and the Fate of Earth, 35–36, 41, 45

THE ROLE OF THE CHURCH: FOSTERING HUMAN-EARTH RELATIONS

When we talk of the role of the Church in the twenty-first century, we must begin with the obvious reality of an industrial civilization ruining the natural world on which we depend for both our physical and our spiritual sustenance. The basic question is no longer human-divine relations; nor, in my view, is it inter-human relations. The basic issue is human-Earth relations. The future of the other two relations depends upon this third relation, our human capacity to recognize our place in the structure of the universe and to fulfill our role within this setting.

What is happening now is something far beyond any historical change or cultural modification that humans have known in the past, changes such as occurred when we moved from the classical to the medieval period or from the medieval world to the Enlightenment period. Both in its modality and in its order of the magnitude what is happening now is something vastly different.

We are changing the chemistry, the geosystems, and the biosystems of the planet on a scale such as has not occurred for the past sixty-five million years, since the beginning of what is known as the Cenozoic era. Already we have terminated this era in its basic creativity. The only viable future for the planet or for ourselves is to recognize the devastation that we have caused and enter a new era that we might think of as the Ecozoic era, a period when humans would be present to the planet in a mutually enhancing manner.

There is one simple cause for the devastating situation in which we find ourselves. We have replaced the universe as the primary referent concerning reality and value in the phenomenal world with the human as the supreme referent of reality and value. We have rejected the divinely established order of the universe and are attempting to establish a contrived human order in its place, under the assumption that we know better than nature how the universe and planet Earth should function. No pathology ever invented could be so perverse and so devastating to the delicate balance of life and existence on this planet.

Along with this distortion of the order of the universe we have broken the unity of the universe and especially of the life systems on Earth. We have established a discontinuity between the nonhuman and the human components of the universe and have given all rights to the human. We have considered the universe as composed of objects to be exploited rather than as subjects to be communed with.

—"The Role of the Church in the Twenty-First Century," in
The Christian Future and the Fate of Earth, 46–47

CHRISTIANITY'S GREAT WORK

At this moment of transition, the twenty-first-century Church, which has lost a sense of its basic purposes in these past centuries, could restore its efficacy and extend its influence over human affairs. The Church could be a powerful force in bringing about the healing of a distraught Earth. The Church could provide an integrating reinterpretation of our new story of the universe. In this manner it could renew religion in its primary expression as celebration, as ecstatic delight in existence. This, I propose, is the Great Work to which Christianity is called in these times.

In relation to its traditional teaching, a new understanding will need to emerge in almost every aspect of belief, discipline, and worship. In most instances this change will lead back to fundamental emphases too long neglected. It should first be observed that our new understanding of the universe through empirical processes and through our instruments of observation has given us an immediacy—even a new intimacy—with the universe in its sacred dimension.

—"The Role of the Church in the Twenty-First Century," in
The Christian Future and the Fate of Earth, 53.

MEMBERS OF
THE EARTH COMMUNITY

Christianity, as well as most other great religions, has been excessively oriented toward transcendence. A true Earth consciousness needs to be developed. Further, not only has divine transcendence been an overwhelming preoccupation, but human transcendence of the natural world has also been also emphasized. Now we need a greater sense of humans, not as transcending the Earth community, but as members of the Earth community. If God has desired to become a member of that community, humans themselves should be willing to accept their status as members of that same Earth community.

—"The Third Mediation," in
The Christian Future and the Fate of Earth, 11.

UNIVERSE AS
SELF-EMERGENT PROCESS

The simple truth is that most of us no longer live in a sacred universe. This lack of a sacred context of existence causes us to feel alienated from and even antagonistic toward the natural world. . . . Even when we view the distant mountains or look out over the oceans or see the stars at night, what we experience is a momentary exaltation of spirit, not the sense of a pervasive divine presence with decisive control over our lives.

My suggestion is that we take a serious look at the universe as it reveals itself to us in this century. We now experience the universe, within the phenomenal order, as a self-emergent process that has gone through a long sequence of irreversible transformations through the millennia to become the world about us. . . .

Discoveries of how the universe, the planet Earth, and we ourselves have come into being have so challenged our Christian understanding that we are still unable, intellectually or emotionally, to feel fully at home in this context. We have little appreciation even of the planet Earth that is unique in our solar system in its ability to bring forth its astounding variety of living beings. In this it is unique among all the planets of our solar system.

We ourselves were brought into being through this process. The universe story and the human story are a single story. We are so intimately associated with the world of the living that we must consider ourselves as cousins to every other living being. Yet, because we are so alienated from the universe in its unfolding reality, we do not appreciate our place or our role in this process. We do not live in a universe at all. We live and function in a cultural tradition, in an economic order, in a world of political allegiance, not in a physical universe or in what we generally refer to as the natural world.

—"The Wisdom of the Cross," in
The Christian Future and the Fate of Earth, 83–84

DETACHMENT FROM THE WORLD

Many people in religious settings who live more intimately with the land have been taught that it is spiritually preferable to keep apart from attachment to this world. Thus in the Advent season we pray that we may "love the things of heaven and judge wisely of the things of Earth." To judge wisely of the things of Earth means to keep a detached stance in order to avoid being emotionally bonded to the magnificent and "seductive" aspects of the planet. During other seasons, we separate out the heavenly world from the earthly world in such a way that this alienation is deepened. The presence of the divine in the natural world is obscured or diminished in our consciousness. Alienation deepens into suspicion and antagonism.

Even when we live in a spiritual universe, it is the ancient universe of our religious imaginations. This is the universe in which our religious traditions took shape, not the universe as we experience it at present. Our alienation from the natural world is paradoxical because the universe in all its grandeur and awesome qualities has generally been considered the primary manifestation of the divine, not only by Christians but also by many other peoples of the world. For example, among the world's indigenous peoples, where coherent communities are still intact, we find that religious imagination in which intimacy with local bioregions and biodiversity frame the sacred in a seamless continuity with all of life's demands. These religious ways are ancient in human social formation. Early stories and myths served to shape humans in creating dynamic life ways in relation to natural processes. Our modern alienation appears to have drawn us away from this deep instinctual patterning with Earth itself. How could this have happened? What intervening forces have pushed aside the wisdom of Earth?

—"The Wisdom of the Cross," in
The Christian Future and the Fate of Earth, 84

WISDOM OF THE CROSS INTERWOVEN WITH THE WISDOM OF THE WORLD

For most Christians the difficulty is that the biblical story is a narrative of human-divine interaction that takes place against the background of a universe that is fixed in its abiding sequence of seasonal renewal. The universe itself has no story except that of its original formation. Afterwards it is a fixed stage upon which the human-divine drama is enacted. This we can observe in the

City of God of Saint Augustine. In this work he tells the story of the world and the divine design for the world. But after the early treatment of creation the entire story is the human story.

While the emergent universe should be experienced as entirely compatible with Christian belief, it has until now been experienced as alien, ancillary, and even contradictory to authentic doctrine. Nowhere do we hear our new story of the universe told as sacred story. This I propose is a central issue involved in the discussion that is before us. How does the wisdom of the cross function in this new context?

The more we understand the universe story as this is now available to us, the more clearly we see that the wisdom of the cross and the wisdom of the universe are two aspects of a single wisdom, that the universe and the cross are integral parts of a single story. Neither is complete without the other. The order of the cross is coherent with the order of the universe. There is ultimately a single wisdom that reaches from end to end mightily and orders all things sweetly.

Redemptive wisdom cannot be alien to creative wisdom. There has been no mistake. When we speak of the wisdom of the cross being adverse to the wisdom of this world, we must understand this as referring to a false wisdom, not to the true wisdom of the universe. This type of insight is not new in Christianity. Indeed, medieval thinkers presented a range of perspectives on cosmology and creation that attempted to integrate their understanding of the wisdom of the cross in relation to the wisdom of the world.

—"The Wisdom of the Cross," in
The Christian Future and the Fate of Earth, 85

PEACE WITH EARTH

This extravagant expectation of a future built on human plundering of Earth's natural resources is largely responsible for the oppression of humans under our modern economic institutions. It is not only natural resources that are involved in this effort but also human resources. The consequence is an ever greater exploitation of the weaker by the stronger, of the less competent by the more competent, of those who own nothing by those who own everything. While such abuse has always occurred in human history, it has become especially critical in these times. We could endure the limitations of life and our human condition more graciously in a human community of shared benefits and burdens. We need only reflect on both the wisdom of the cross and the wisdom of the universe, namely, that sacrifice with each other and for each other is a dimension of life itself and should lead to an expansion rather than to a diminishment of life for each of us.

So too with ethnic differences. We have never learned the wisdom of the universe, a wisdom that teaches that difference is a primary condition for there even being a universe. It is also the reason why Saint Thomas speaks in the *Summa Theologica* (I, q. 47, a. 1) of difference as "the perfection of the universe." The racial and cultural diversity among the peoples of Earth is among the greatest splendors of Earth. Each ethnic group and each culture is enhanced rather than diminished by the manner in which the distinctive qualities of each group increase the grandeur of all the others. Finally, I would suggest that there is need for peace with Earth if there is to be peace among the peoples of Earth. Our alienation from Earth is one of the most significant causes of our alienation from each other.

We are now entering a new period in the religious-cultural history of our Christian-derived civilization. In this new period there is some doubt about the next generations being religious in the sense that prior generations have been religious according to Christian doctrinal or ethical imperatives. Nor can we expect that in secularized society the coming generations will be religious out of any scriptural basis for their thinking. The sacred writings that guided us are unlikely to guide those so extensively alienated from traditions that we have known. In such a situation there is a need for something beyond a sacred book that teaches the spiritual wisdom of the cross. What is needed, I suggest, is the additional wisdom of the universe. There is a need of sanctions other than the spiritual sanctions indicated by Christian belief. I suggest that there is a need for the wisdom of a universe that can impose physical sanctions upon whomever violates its laws, a universe that establishes the conditions of life itself.

The experience of our generation is a parable that future generations might well consider. Because we have violated the conditions of life by our assault on the planet, the planet is withdrawing the pure air and water and the fertility of the soil. The immense shoals of fish that once flourished in the oceans are no longer there. The exuberance of life that once existed on the planet can no longer be found. Nature cannot endure the afflictions we impose on it. We will obey the divine directions of the natural world or we will die. This is the ultimate imperative from which there is no escape.

Just what the future might be we cannot know with any clarity. We should at least be able to see that the wisdom of the cross presented in opposition to the wisdom of the universe cannot be an effective answer to the difficulties that we confront at the present time. We might also be able to see that our new story of the universe should be understood as a sacred story in which divine mysteries are revealed to us with a clarity that we have never before known. Finally, we might want to consider that we are just now at a unique moment when the wisdom of the cross, in this new context, can arrive at a more expanded expression of itself.

—"The Wisdom of the Cross," in
The Christian Future and the Fate of Earth, 94–95

DIVINE INDWELLING

To preserve this sacred world of our origins from destruction, our great need is for renewal of the entire Western religious-spiritual tradition in relation to the integral functioning of the biosystems of planet Earth. We need to move from a spirituality of alienation from the natural world to a spirituality of intimacy with it, from a spirituality of the divine as revealed in verbal revelation to a spirituality of the divine as revealed in the visible world about us, from a spirituality concerned with justice simply to humans to a justice that includes the larger Earth community. . . .

We cannot save ourselves without saving the world in which we live. There are not two worlds, the world of the human and a world of the other modes of being. There is a single world. We will live or die as this world lives or dies. We can say this both physically and spiritually. We will be spiritually nourished by this world or we will be starved for spiritual nourishment. No other revelatory experience can do for the human what the experience of the natural world does.

When we try to understand the universe and our place in it, we find ourselves doubly estranged, not only from the universe of Genesis but also from the universe as we now know it through empirical observation and scientific insight. Spiritually we may feel ourselves at home with the Genesis story. Yet, as regards understanding the evolution of the universe, its emergence into being, the sequence of transformations through which it has passed, and the manner of its functioning, Genesis cannot enlighten us. At the same time, the scientific story of the universe, such as we now know it, is communicated to us as merely material in its substance, mechanistic in its functioning, and random in its development.

Once we get beyond the explanation given by scientists, however, and look at data derived from their intense observation of the universe over these past few centuries, we begin to see a story of immense significance, a story that reveals the deepest mysteries if only we know how to understand the story. We now perceive the universe as having come into being from an original flaring forth of primordial energy, then passing through a sequence of irreversible transformation episodes that have brought into being the visible world about us.

This phenomenal universe that we observe in such detailed scientific fashion cannot be explained simply in itself. In every way it is dependent on a numinous, transphenomenal, divine creative power. When we explain the universe as we now know the universe in its originating moments and its long sequence of transformations, we are explaining the manner in which the Creator has brought the universe into being. Yet, we must recognize that the universe is not a puppet creation manipulated by some transcendent power. Such a creation would not satisfy the purposes of creation such as we know these to be. The created being would not have the independence needed to enter into an intimate divine-human relationship. Such a being could not freely offer divine praise. For these reasons, the divine creates a phenomenal world with the power to develop greater complexity through emergent processes. The wonderful thing about the universe is that it constitutes an absolute unity in which each component is universe-referent and all the components are inter-referent among themselves.

This universe, which we must now understand as our sacred universe, is the same universe that is presented in the Book of Genesis. It is a universe, however, that is experienced through immediate empirical observation rather than simply through the inspired words of a narrator writing in a distant region and an ancient time in a strange language. Through this observational process we have also come to know the universe as an emergent process over an immense period of time. Once this emergent reality is seen within a religious and spiritual context, once it becomes clear that the universe itself has a spiritual dimension from the beginning, then we have the basis for a new cosmology in which we can find new depths of meaning in biblical truths. . . .

Thus the basic Christian understanding of the universe is one in which the human community and the natural world are seen as a unified, single community with an overarching purpose: the exaltation and joy of existence, praise of the divine, and participation in the great liturgy of the universe. Every element in Christian belief and moral teaching, every aspect of our sacramental system, of our patterns of worship, and of our spirituality depend on the world about us. Indeed, the natural world is the primary revelation to us of the divine. Once we accept the universe as an emergent reality, then what is said in Genesis, in the Psalms, in the writings of Saint John, in the Epistle to the Colossians, can be said of the universe as we now perceive it. This understanding expands rather than contracts our understanding of scriptural and theological statements.

In this emergent process we recognize transformation moments as those instants when the numinous presence in the phenomenal world manifests itself with special clarity. These moments include the time of a supernova explosion that produced the ninety-some elements needed for the solar system, for planet Earth, for life and consciousness. These transformation events can be considered cosmological moments of grace. Just as there are historical moments of grace and sacramental moments of grace, so, too, there are such cosmological moments. These are times that deserve ritual commemoration, just as moments in the annual solar cycle do; solstice and spring equinox are given ritual expression in nativity and resurrection liturgies. In most religious traditions, diurnal moments of transformation, dawn and dusk, the mysterious transition from day to night and from night today are profoundly religious moments to be observed with appropriate prayer and ritual. . . .

We are in the process of losing the beauty and wonder of a gracious world designed in some manner as the place where the meeting of the divine and the human can be achieved in its full expression, a place suitable for the divine indwelling. Will we have the energy and the will to restore this world?

—"Christianity and Ecology," in
*The Christian Future
and the Fate of Earth*, 63–67

STORY OF THE UNIVERSE

All of this must find its expression in the story of the universe. Indeed, the various civilizations of the world are generally founded in some story indicating how things came into being in the beginning, how they came to be as they are, and the role of the human in the story. This story of the universe is eventually the context of education, of healing, and of any other activity in which humans engage.

This story is the story that the universe tells of itself. It is the story told by every being in the universe, by the stars in the heavens, by the mountains and rivers of Earth, by every wind that blows, by every snowflake that falls, by every leaf in the forest. To know this story of the universe as our sacred story is to have an adequate foundation for the task before us. This story tells us who we are and how we came to be here and what our lives are all about.

For the Christian it tells us of the Trinity in the three most basic tendencies of the universe: differentiation, interiority, and universal bonding. These deepest tendencies of the universe, which manifest the ultimate divine forces that brought the world into being, can provide us with a profound way of thinking about Father, Son, and Holy Spirit. So, too, the universe story can be told as the Christ story in accord with the teaching of so many Church Fathers, as well as theologians and spiritual teachers over the centuries. . . .

This is because as Christians we have been primarily concerned with divine human and interhuman affairs in accord with the two great commandments, love of God and love of neighbor. Thus we have fulfilled the precepts of the law and the prophets. However effective this presentation of Christian spiritual teaching might have been in the past, it is no longer sufficiently comprehensive for Christian survival. There is a third component that cannot be neglected, namely, love of the natural world, without which the human world cannot function in any effective manner. The entire Earth was born of divine love and will survive only through our human and Christian love. Christians are ineffective just now largely because we have not understood the need of compassion for suffering Earth, the compassion expressed by Saint Paul in his reference to the world "groaning for deliverance" (Rom. 8:22).

At the present time, the protest of the pillage of Earth, the compassion for Earth, and the commitment to the preservation of Earth are left mainly to secular environmental organizations as though the matter were too peripheral to be of concern to Christians.

—"Women Religious: Voices of Earth," in
The Christian Future and the Fate of Earth, 81, 71.

CHRISTIAN COSMOLOGY

As Christians, the question of human-Earth relations seems outside our concern. So overwhelming are our religious and social concerns that we fail to recognize that both our social and our religious well-being largely depend on the well-being of Earth, which provides sustenance for our physical, imaginative, and emotional as well as our religious well-being. To understand planet Earth and our intimate relationship with it, we need to know the great story of Earth and of the universe that brought it and ourselves into being.

What needs to be recognized is that this new story of the universe represents the greatest change in human thought and consciousness since the rise of the neolithic period. Thus it is not only a difficulty for Christians, it is a difficulty for human consciousness throughout the Earth community. One of the reasons for this problem is that the new story of the universe has brought with it such enormous powers that we are presently engaged not simply in historical or cultural change; we are changing the chemistry of the planet, its biological systems, and even its geological structure. In each of these areas, the human presence in the twentieth century has brought about a profoundly disturbed situation. The human has become not the crowning glory of Earth, but its most destructive presence.

The solution is not, then, a case of simply restoring a former religious, spiritual, moral, or humanist tradition. It is a case of reordering the human in its entire relationship with the planet on which we live, a mission for which Christians are not especially suited, since we have seldom shown any extensive regard for the creation process, dedicated as we have been since the thirteenth century to a primarily redemptive task.

—"Christian Cosmology," in
The Christian Future and the Fate of Earth, 27–28

CHANGING A GEOLOGICAL ERA

First we should discuss the order of magnitude of the events taking place in our times. What is happening in our times is not just another historical transition or simply another cultural change. The devastation of the planet that we are bringing about is negating some hundreds of millions, even billions, of years of past development on Earth. This is a most momentous period of change, a change unparalleled in the four and a half billion years of Earth history.

Even as we reflect on what is happening, we need to reflect also on who we are and why we are faced with such a momentous issue. All indications suggest that we are, in a sense, a chosen group, a chosen generation, or a chosen human community. We did not ask to be here at this time. We were destined to be here at this time in the sense that the time of our lives is determined for us. Some of the prophets, when asked to undertake certain missions, said, "Don't choose me; that's too much for me." God says, "You are going anyway." We are not asked whether we wish to live at this particular time. We are here. The inescapable is before us.

My generation has lived through a large part of this momentous period of change. Public radio did not exist when I was born. To have gone through all the discoveries of science, to have seen the planet change as much as it has been changed, is stupendous. But we have changed not simply the human, not simply Western civilization, not simply the North American world, we have changed the very structure of the planet. We have changed the chemistry of the planet, the biosystems of the planet, even the geology of the planet. Now we are changing the ozone layer, and bringing about what is called the greenhouse effect.

Events in this modality and at this order of magnitude have never taken place in the total course of human history, possibly in the course of Earth history. There have been significant moments of extinction at the end of the Paleozoic era, some 220 million years ago, and also sixty-five million years ago at the end of the Mesozoic era. But now we are in the terminal phase of the Cenozoic era, a period when many of the developments of the past sixty-five million years are being extinguished. We are not capable of extinguishing everything, but we are wreaking severe damage on the Earth process. We have even set in motion forces that are extinguishing many of the major life systems that have come into being during the Cenozoic period.

We could call this Cenozoic period, the last sixty-five million years, the "lyric" period of Earth history. During this period, we have the full development of the flowers; we have the wondrous development of the birds and the insects. Many of these living forms existed before the beginning of the Cenozoic era, but they had their full flowering only in the past 65 million years. Then we humans came into being. What we are doing is setting a reversed sequence of forces into operation. The whole Cenozoic process is to some extent being negated. What is happening is on *this* order of magnitude. What is happening is not simply something that is happening to the Western world, nor is it happening simply to the human. It is happening on a planetary scale.

All the human modalities of being that have existed in the past are being profoundly altered. We ourselves are being changed. Christianity, which came into being some two thousand years ago, and our biblical revelation, which began some thirty-five hundred years ago, must now function within this context at this order of magnitude. Unfortunately, there is no indication so far that Christians are beginning to think of this scale of change. Just as the planet is changing more than it has changed in such a long period of time, so the human order that brought about this change is being called to alter itself in an equally profound way.

That is why I suggest that what is happening now to Christian theology, or any theology or any religious life or any moral code, is the most profound change that has taken place during the past five thousand years. All human affairs are forced to change more than they have changed, certainly since the larger civilizations came into being.

We can even say that all the civilizations and religious traditions, which began generally five thousand years ago, have accomplished a major part of their historical mission. This includes Christian civilization. This transformation includes the total religious experience of the human. It includes all experience of the human. We can never do without these accomplishments. They will have a major role in shaping the future. But they have to change on an order in which they have never changed before. One perspective on these transformations comes from Teilhard de Chardin (1881–1955), who places the human in the vast unfolding processes of evolution.

Sometimes I say it this way: The traditional religions in themselves and out of their existing resources cannot deal with the problems that we have to deal with, but we cannot deal with these problems without the traditions. They cannot do it within their own resources as they exist at the present time, but it cannot be done without them. Something new has been added, a new experience, a new context, and we must now function out of this new context. We cannot deductively get our guidance from the past. There is, in a sense, a new revelatory experience that has given us a new sense of the universe, a new sense of the planet Earth, a new sense of life, of the human, even a new sense of being Christian. We have, in a sense, a new revelatory experience of the divine through our present understanding of the time-developmental universe.

The universe story is the quintessence of reality. We perceive the story. We put it in our language, the birds put it in theirs, and the trees put it in theirs. We can read the story of the universe in the trees. Everything tells the story of the universe. The winds tell the story of the universe, literally, not just imaginatively. The story has its imprint everywhere, and that is why it is so important to know the story. If you do not know the story, in a certain sense you do not know yourself; you do not know anything.

—"The Divine and Our Present Revelatory Moment,"
in *Befriending the Earth*, 4–7

EPIC OF EVOLUTION

In this evolutionary story, we easily identify the moments of change. These moments of transformation are the mysterious, the sacred moments, the moments when a numinous guidance shows through amid the turbulent course of universe affairs. Such moments we can no longer believe are controlled by purely random consequences out of a rolling sea of conflicting forces. Between the random and the directed, as the geneticist Theodore Dobzhansky insisted, lies the creative. Randomness is another name for the mysterious ordering processes that affect all artistic creativity.

The dazzling course of things is exciting indeed. Yet the mysterious moment when the galactic formations took shape and the stars were formed throughout the heavens deserves celebration in liturgies not dissimilar from the liturgies coordinating human activities with the transforming moments of the seasons of the year or the transformation of day into night or night into day.

To illustrate how the Epic of Evolution might be integrated into traditional religious services, I would like to mention the most sacred moment in traditional Christian liturgy, the moment designated as the Easter vigil. This is the moment when the experience of life renewal is reenacted. This liturgy is to be celebrated in the darkness of night, just before the dawn. At this moment, the story of the creation of the world is recited, as are the events that transpired in the historical order until the moment of renewal. What is striking in this narrative is that the story of creation is a very limited narrative, since in earlier times the only account of creation of the universe in the religious traditions of the Western world was contained in the few paragraphs of the Book of Genesis. After that, the entire story of history was the human story. There was no further story of the galaxies or the formation of Earth or the evolutionary emergence of life. What is now available to us is a more extensive account of the universe and how it came into being through the immense amount of time and through a long sequence of transformation episodes. This, to my mind, needs to be incorporated into the story of the creation of the world as this is narrated in religious liturgy.

Of the possible moments for celebration, one that deserves mention is the galactic formation and the formation of the stars. Another might be the first-generation star that, some four and a half billion years ago, formed the ninety-some elements in its supernova moment of implosion, and then explosion, as fragments into space. By gathering these fragments with the aid of gravitational attraction, our own star came into being, with the Earth as one of its nine planets. We might note the rise of the first living cell that became possible some three billion years ago amid the turbulent shaping of the planet. Then came sexual reproduction, later photosynthesis. From then on, a long choice of celebrations would present itself.

The evolutionary responsibility of the human, from a religious perspective, is to perceive the epic of the universe as the primary revelatory experience of our times. . . .The natural world is the irreversible sequence of change such as we now experience it through empirical scientific studies. There is an additional revelation that we are having. Revelation is not something merely of the past. It is the reality of the present. Just as the universe reveals the basic sources of economic understanding, as the universe is the guide to medical understanding, so the universe is our guide to understanding the sacred dimension of the universe. For too long a time we have refused to accept the insight into the world of the sacred that is there before us. The scientists themselves have been overwhelmed by their discoveries and have found it difficult to explain themselves in other than scientific equations and mathematical description.

Now that this awareness of the epic dimension of the evolutionary process begins to be seriously considered, a new world of understanding begins to appear on the horizon. My first thought is that we not try to write theology at this moment. My thought is that we celebrate the glory of the universe that is there before us. We need have no doubt of the appropriateness of our celebration of the sacred in this epic narrative. Here we join the great wisdom of traditions of the past. In the Epic of Evolution, science becomes a path to wisdom.

—"The Epic of Evolution," in *Evening Thoughts*, 123–25

A COSMOLOGICAL UNDERSTANDING OF THE TRINITY

It should be immediately evident that this threefold tendency provides a remarkable model for understanding the Christian doctrine of the Trinity. We have the family model presented in the Bible as Father, Son, and Holy Spirit. We have the psychological model presented by Augustine as intellect reflecting on itself. We have the social model sometimes used in modern times as the self, the other, the community. Yet none of these examples has the special quality of the cosmological model which present the Father as the principle of differentiation; the Son as the icon, the Word, the principle of inner articulation; the Holy Spirit as the bonding force holding all things together in a creative, compassionate embrace. In this context the Church should have little difficulty understanding the universe as the primary sacred community.

In a similar manner the incarnation can be seen in a cosmological context. Here we find a profound way in which our new understanding of the universe provides an unsuspected depth of insight into incarnation in accord with the teachings of Saint Paul in the Epistle to the Colossians and Saint John in the preface to his Gospel. Neither of these scriptural writers saw the Christ figure simply as an individual. The Christ event was of cosmic dimensions, requiring a cosmic as well as individual mode of being. This is why Saint Paul tells us that in Christ all things hold together. In like manner, John begins his Gospel not immediately with the human birth of Christ, but with the Eternal Christ as the creative Logos of the Universe.

If we understand the Christ reality to have a cosmic aspect, so we must consider that the universe has a Christ aspect. This is the Christian mode of understanding the universe itself in terms of the human form. This sense of cosmic person is extensively used in the traditions of various civilizations. It occurs with special clarity in the Buddhist world with the cosmic or ontological dimension of the Buddha figure. It occurs in the *Mahapurusha* (Great Person) concept of Hinduism, as well as in the concept of the one body of the universe in the Chinese tradition. Amazingly, this sense of cosmic person occurs in the most advanced modes of interpretation of the universe as expressed by modern physics. There it is spoken of as the "cosmological anthropic principle." In this context, the relationship between the human mind that knows the universe is considered in its relation to the universe whence the human mind comes into being. . . .

The role of the Church in the twenty-first century, then, is to speak more directly concerning the universe itself as the primordial revelation of the divine. It should be clear that verbal revelation cannot be a primary revelation, since any communication that takes place through language takes on the distortions of the language, the particular social forms of the times, and the complex patterns of historical events occurring during that period. In contrast, the revelation of the natural world directly and immediately awakens a sense of awe and mystery along with a sense of creatureliness. It arouses, as well, a tendency to worship.

Until recently, Christians have been concerned with the soul, the inner life, spiritual disciplines, sacramental participation, works of mercy, and care for the impoverished—activities all leading to salvation in a trans-earthly realm. However unfortunate the loss of the natural world in all its grandeur, this, they contended, was not essential to the spiritual salvation of the soul. It was merely the realm of the secular naturalist or the mechanistic scientist. In this manner, the discontinuity between the human and the nonhuman was profoundly affirmed within Christianity.

To counter this tendency we need a more adequate understanding of the universe, of how it came into being, of its governing tendencies, and of the sequence of transformations whereby it has taken on its present forms of expression. We need to know how the solar system and Earth came into being, how life developed on the planet, and, finally, how we ourselves appeared and what our human role has been within this amazing process. All these things need to be understood as aspects of a spiritual as well as a physical process. Only such comprehensive and deep understanding can restore the integral functioning of planet Earth upon which human well-being depends. This is the fundamental task of the Church in the twenty-first century.

—"The Role of the Church in the Twenty-First Century," in
The Christian Future and the Fate of Earth, 56–58

THE DIVINE:
THE ULTIMATE MYSTERY OF THINGS

There are five basic subjects that have been selected for consideration in this unit: God, the Trinity, the role of the human, creation, and revelation. In a certain sense, these all come together: the sense of God, of the human, of creation, and revelation. We cannot deal with these separately. We would have no sense of the divine without creation. Speculatively, we could talk about God as being prior to or outside creation or independent of creation but in actual fact there is no such being as God without creation. When a person associates the creation with the divine, it is the existential fact that there is no God without creation and there is no creation without God.

As a note here, I would like to mention something that comes up constantly. I do not generally use the word "God" because I think the word has been overused. It is used in so many different ways that it carries too much ambivalence. Also, I wish to address myself to people of any belief, so I try to use words that make sense to everybody. In my writings generally, I am concerned primarily with the larger society, not simply with Christians or even "religious" people.

The term "God" refers to the ultimate mystery of things, something beyond that which we can understand adequately. It is experienced as the Great Spirit by many of the indigenous peoples of the world. The Great Spirit is the all-pervasive, mysterious power that is present and observed in the rising and setting of the sun, in the growing of living things, in the sequence of the seasons. This mysterious power carries things through to their brilliant expression in all the forms that we observe in the world about us, in the stars at night, in the feel and experience of the wind, in the surging expanse of the oceans. Peoples generally experience an awesome, stupendous presence that cannot be expressed adequately in human words. Since it cannot be expressed in language, people often dance this experience, they express in it music, in art, in the pervasive of the beautiful throughout the whole of daily life, in the laughter of children, in the taste of bread, in the sweetness of an apple. At every moment we are experiencing the overwhelming mystery of existence. It is that simple but that ineffable. What is the divine? It is the ineffable, pervasive presence in the world about us.

One of the things that we have to recognize is that this divine presence in creation is understood differently in our new historical context. Originally, the divine was perceived as manifested throughout the world, throughout the total range of natural phenomena; it was simply a given. There was a spatial experience of the divine manifestation in the natural world. That is, time moved in ever-renewing, seasonal cycles of change. It was eternal. The universe existed as it always was and always would be.

In the biblical world, however, a new sense of history came into being, an awareness that the universe emerged into being at a definite moment. Before that, human consciousness awakened to the universe as the universe always was, always would be, in ever-renewing cycles. Humans could not really interfere with that or change it. They could not begin it, nor could they end it.

—"The Divine and Our Present Revelatory Moment," in *Befriending the Earth*, 10–11

CONSCIOUSNESS AND COMMUNITY

Now we have something different in our experience of the universe. We perceive the universe through a new mode of intellectual perception. Earlier, what was involved was immediate intuitive experience: we simply observed the natural world around us. More recently, however, we have begun to look at the natural world in terms of empirical science, with the aid of microscopic and telescopic instruments. We have looked at the universe very intensely, studying the stars, for example, trying to find out how they came into being. We have looked at the world about us and have analyzed the elements until we see how things grow. Gradually, we have come to understand that the universe is not simply a given, and that it did indeed have a beginning in time. Time, we discover, is irreversible. The sequence in the larger arc of its development has been from lesser to greater complexity and consciousness.

Our modern scientific view of the universe thus coincides with the biblical realm rather than the nonbiblical world, which does not have such a clear sense of an emergent universe that began at a definitive historical moment. As we count back into the ages, we discover that our universe has existed for a vast period of time. Presently, we can calculate something like fourteen billion years. This understanding of the universe, however, is different from many previous understandings. It is historical, rather than metaphysical, time. In India, for example, the universe (as traditionally understood) comes into being over some trillions of years, to exist for trillions of years, and then is extinguished, only to come back again and again. This view represents a kind of metaphysical time, and is not based on an empirical study of the material cosmos and its history.

The Chinese, on the other hand, have what I would call chronological time in human history. They can tell better than any other people of the world what happened in their history three thousand years ago. They know with a great deal of precision just what was happening then. This I describe as chronological history. Meaningful history, that is, the story of meaningful developmental time, comes into being with the revelatory experience in the Middle East, which was developed in the biblical world and the Christian world. Even with Christians, the universe itself was viewed in an ever-continuing, seasonal time perspective—although the very essence of Christianity is developmental *human* time, the working out of a divine presence in the human world in terms of the kingdom of God. What we have now, through our modern story of the universe, is a new sense of a universe, one that had a precise beginning and has gone through a sequence of differentiating transformations leading from lesser to greater complexity and greater modes of consciousness. These two need, in some manner, to be related, an ascending universe of consciousness and the rise of spiritual community. The universe itself is the most basic expression of community. The universe is the ultimate sacred community.

The beginning of the universe, we now see, was not a homogenous smudge, but, rather, involved articulated energy constellations bound together in an inseparable unity. The various parts of the universe are outwardly differentiated, inwardly articulated, and bonded together in a comprehensive intimacy of every particle with every other particle. There is something very important about the beginning of the universe as we now know it. I consider this revelatory in a magnificent way, because it tells us something about the powers that brought the universe into being at the beginning.

—"The Divine and Our Present Revelatory Moment,"
in *Befriending the Earth*, 11–13

THE CURVATURE OF SPACE

In the beginning, we have this expansive force, a differentiating force. We have the articulated entities that come into being and this takes place shortly after the primordial radiation. Immediately, gravitation comes into being and things are pulled together in a profound intimacy. So we have two forces at the beginning of the universe. We have the emergent diversification process, a kind of explosion process, and then we have a containing process. The attraction that everything has for everything else is most important. Nobody knows what this attraction is. Isaac Newton (1642–1727), who wrote the laws of gravitation, said he did not know what it was at all. He gave the laws for this attraction, but he did not know what it was, and nobody to this day can tell you what gravitation is. But we do know that this attractive force and this explosive force constitute what is called the curvature of the universe. Everything that exists comes into existence within this context, the curvature of space. If this rate of emergence had been a trillionth of a fraction faster or a trillionth of a fraction slower, the universe would have either exploded or collapsed. It had to be precise to the trillion trillionth of a margin. Why? Because this curvature of the universe had to be such that the universe could continue expanding and yet neither explode nor collapse. So we have a universe held together, but not held so tightly that its expansion or its creativity would be stifled. If the attraction overcame the expansion, it would collapse. But if the expansion overcame the attraction, then it would explode.

I call this curvature of space "the compassionate curve" of the universe, or the compassionate curve that *embraces* the universe. What do we do when we meet one another? We reach out and embrace one another. That embrace reflects the curvature of the universe. We talk about reflexive thinking on the part of the human mind because we are that being in whom the universe reflects on itself. What is that reflection? That is the expression in human intelligence of the curvature of the universe. It is the curvature of the universe coming back upon itself. There would be no human reflection if it were not for that curvature. There would be no human affection without gravitational attraction. Gravitation, built into this process, binds everything together so closely that nothing can ever be separated from anything else. Alienation is an impossibility, a cosmological impossibility. We can *feel* alienated, but we can never *be* alienated.

The other thing that is so important in this process is the relationship of origin. Everything in the universe is genetically cousin to everything else. There is literally one family, one bonding, in the universe, because everything is descended from the same source. In this creative process, all things come into being. On the planet Earth, all living things are clearly derived from a single origin. We are literally born as a community; the trees, the birds, and all living creatures are bonded together in a single community of life. This again gives us a sense that we belong. Community is not something that we dream up or think would be nice. Literally, we are a single community. The planet Earth is a single community of existence, and we exist in this context.

—"The Divine and Our Present Revelatory Moment,"
in *Befriending the Earth*, 13–15

8

Ecozoic Era

Thomas Berry's awareness of the magnitude of the planetary change we have effected with our industrial revolution was one of his great insights. Indeed, he saw that the Cenozoic period, the last sixty-five million years of the incredible florescence of life on Earth, is coming to an end. This is due to the extinction spasm that humans have induced. Such a realization provoked Berry to call for a transformation into a new period of flourishing for the Earth community, which he termed the Ecozoic era.

The Cenozoic period provided the biological context for self-reflexive consciousness to emerge. The richness of life evident in this period has given rise to the human capacity for wonder, beauty, and intimacy. In presenting the term "Ecozoic," Berry calls for a new awareness and reciprocity on the part of humans so they can be "present to the planet in a mutually enhancing manner."

This shift to the Ecozoic occurs just as contemporary geologists are identifying our current age as the "Anthropocene," namely, the period in which human-induced change is the defining characteristic. Berry understands that the transformation needed now is a turn from an anthropocentric perspective to biocentric and ecocentric concerns. The full resilience of Earth's ecosystems is beyond our knowledge. Nonetheless, life as we know it is being severely curtailed by human industrial obsessions that distract us from realizing the consequences of what we are doing.

Even religions themselves are threatened as we diminish our sense of experiencing the divine in nature. However, the religions show little sign of appreciating how such a sense of the divine arises within the landscape of Earth. We are being confronted by the critical, moral dilemmas presented by suicide, homocide, and even genocide. But, as Berry observes, we have yet to hear the world religions speak about the impinging challenges of biocide and geocide. These present powerful moral concerns regarding the diminishment of life throughout the planet, as well as the imperilment of the ecosphere itself.

Berry meditates on the spiritual realization of this reality in his reflection on the human story as integral with the universe from the beginning. The dynamic presence of the universe to itself is reflected in human consciousness—in the galactic story and the Earth story that infuses every dimension of our universe, interrelating it to everything else. Perfection is simultaneously in the whole and that whole is expressed in each particular being and event of the universe. Languages may vary in their efforts to articulate reality as event, being, or relationship, but many languages articulate the profound kinship of emergence that now comes to us as life.

One articulation that has arisen out of the Western world is the term, "wild," which Berry described as the spontaneities of life. Rather than simply idiosyncratic or individuated, socially constructed or biologically determined, he understands these spontaneities as profound expressions of the universe within each particular being. Wild, for Berry, is not something subject to uncontrollable emotions or driven by unconscious desires, but rather is a subjectivity that is aware of its vibrant place in ecosystems and human communities. It is from this perspective that Berry articulates the determining features of the Ecozoic era as a meditation on that spiritual journey of recovering the wild.

THE EARTH COMMUNITY

The magnitude of the ecological crisis of our times is such that we are presently terminating the Cenozoic era of Earth's development and entering into the Ecozoic era of the Earth process. The Cenozoic has been the period of the expansion of life in the full brilliance of its expression, but this expansion of the life systems of Earth is being terminated. This will affect all our human institutions and professions that were appropriate to the Cenozoic era. They must now undergo a transformation if they are to be integral with the new period in the historical evolution of the planet. The transformation required is a transformation from an anthropocentric norm of reality and value to a biocentric or geocentric norm. This will affect every aspect of our human thought and action. It will affect language, religion, morality, economics, education, science, technology, and medicine.

In our discussion of sacred community, we need to understand that in all our activities Earth is primary, the human is derivative. The Earth is our primary community. Indeed, all particular modes of earthly being exist by virtue of their role within this community.

—"Earth as Sacred Community," in *Evening Thoughts*, 43

THE DAWN OF THE ECOZOIC ERA

Humans as a planetary presence are currently terminating the Cenozoic era of Earth history and entering the Ecozoic era. This geological shift is marked by the fact that the sixth extinction spasm is occurring, and it is of our own making. . . . The survival of other species and the vitality of human affairs will depend on our capacity to adapt to this transition. Above all, this entry into the Ecozoic era is the entry into the period of the Earth community with a new sense of its sacred dimension. . . .

Presently, those of us who are heirs to the biblical tradition are trying to be religious in accordance with written scriptures and covenant relations with the divine based on a juridic model. This can be effective only as long as it functions within the awesome awakening to the divine evoked by our experience of the natural world. We become religious by fulfilling our role within the larger community of the universe itself. The natural world is both the primary source of religious understanding and the primary religious community. In the natural world, we discover the mysterious power whence all things come into being. In humans this religious community reflects on and celebrates itself and its numinous origins in a special mode of conscious self-awareness.

Rather than accord with these vast cosmic forces in the natural rhythms of their expression, especially in the biosystems of the planet, we have, in recent centuries, been subverting these forces. We have long been imposing our mechanistic patterns on these biosystems, forcing the natural rhythms of Earth to accord with our accelerated demands. When organic processes are too slow or too limited in bringing forth their produce, we force the growth through chemical processes that increase the volume of production, even though the nourishing quality of the product is inferior and the fertility of the land diminished. In a multitude of different ways, we seek to subdue Earth to our own ephemeral purposes, considering this the proper human relationship to the natural world.

Because of this distortion in our thinking, we are carrying out what may be one of the most devastating assaults ever on Earth in more than four billion years of life on this planet. . . .

Not simply the human future is involved. The future of every living being on the planet is at issue. The fate of the planet itself in its most profound physical and psychic structure is being determined. We are witnessing nothing less than the dissolution of the planet Earth and all its living systems in consequence of this strange distortion of our human role in the Earth process that has emerged from within our modern Western world, which was itself born out of a biblical-classical matrix.

—"Earth as Sacred Community," in
Evening Thoughts, 45–47

IF WE LIVED ON THE MOON

Here we might observe that our Western religious institutions are strangely indifferent to what is happening. This indifference arises, apparently, as a result of excessive concern for redemptive processes out of this world—which is considered to be seductive—rather than integration within this world considered to be sacred. There seems to be little realization that the disintegration of the natural world is the destruction of the primordial self-manifestation of the divine. The very existence of religion is threatened in proportion as the splendor of the natural world is diminished. We have a magnificent sense of the divine because we live in such a resplendent world. If we lived on the moon, our sense of the divine would be as dull as the lunar landscape.

Even when we try to bring religious influence to bear on these issues, we find that our religious traditions have little relevance to what is happening. Our Western religions exist in a different world, a world of covenant relations with the divine, a world little concerned with the natural environment or with the Earth community. Our sacred community is seen primarily as one concerned with human-divine relations, with little attraction toward a shared community existence within the larger world of the living. Our iconoclasm is such that we can hardly think of ourselves within a multispecies community or consider that this community of the natural world is the primary locus for the meeting of the divine and the human.

—"Earth as Sacred Community," in
Evening Thoughts, 47–48

NO MORAL TEACHINGS
FOR BIOCIDE OR GEOCIDE

From these observations we can say that establishing a mutually enhancing human presence upon Earth has been a difficulty from the late Paleolithic era until the present. Also, we can say that the biblical-Christian-classical tradition has intensified this alienation from the natural world and has set up conditions that have permitted extensive plundering of Earth for human use. As regards our own specifically Western responsibilities, we must note that, although we have developed a moral teaching concerned with suicide, homicide, and genocide, we have developed no effective teachings concerned with biocide, the killing of the life systems of Earth, or geocide, the killing of Earth itself.

—"Earth as Sacred Community,")in
Evening Thoughts, 52

UNIVERSE AS PRIMARY SACRED COMMUNITY

My proposal is that we cannot fully remedy this situation except by a realization that the universe from the beginning has been a psychic-spiritual, as well as physical-material, reality. Within this context, the human activates one of the deepest dimensions of the universe and is, thus, integral with the universe from its beginning. The universe story needs to be accepted simultaneously as the human story and the story of every being in the universe.

There is a need for the religious traditions, on their part, to appreciate that the primary sacred community is the universe itself, and that every other community becomes sacred by participation in this primary community. The story of the universe is the new sacred story. The Genesis story, however valid in its basic teaching, is no longer adequate for our spiritual needs. We cannot renew the world through the Genesis story; at the same time, we cannot renew the world without including the Genesis story and all those creation stories that have nourished the various segments of the human community through the centuries. These belong to the great story, the sacred story, as we presently know this sacred community.

The new story of the universe is a biospiritual story as well as a galactic story and an Earth story. Above all, the universe as we now know it is integral with itself throughout its vast extent in space and throughout the long series of its transformations in time. Everywhere, at all times, and in each of its particular manifestations, the universe is present to itself. Each atomic element is immediately influencing and being influenced by every other atom of the universe. Nothing can ever be separated from anything else. The Earth is a single if highly differentiated community. This is the quintessential way of understanding the universe.

So, too, every part of the universe activates a particular dimension or aspect of the universe in a unique and unrepeatable manner. Thus everything is needed. Without the perfection of each part, something is lacking from the whole. Each particular being in the universe is needed by the entire universe. With this understanding of our profound kinship with all life, we can establish the basis for a flourishing Earth community.

—"Earth as Sacred Community," in
Evening Thoughts, 57–58

THE WILD AND THE SACRED

To understand the human role in the functioning of Earth, we need to appreciate the spontaneities found in every form of existence in the natural world, spontaneities that we associate with the wild—that which is uncontrolled by human dominance. We misconceive our role if we consider that our historical mission is to "civilize" or to "domesticate" the planet, as though wildness is something destructive rather than the ultimate creative modality of any form of earthly being. We are not here to control. We are here to become integral with the larger Earth community. The community itself and each of its members has ultimately a wild component, a creative spontaneity that is its deepest reality, its most profound mystery.

We might reflect on this sense of the wild and the civilized when the dawn appears through the morning mist. At such times a stillness pervades the world—a brooding sense, a quiet transition from night into day. This experience is deepened when evening responds to morning, as day fades away, and night comes in the depth of its mystery. We are most aware at such moments of transition that the world around us is beyond human control. So too are the transition phases of human life; at birth, maturity, and death we brood over our presence in a world of mystery far greater than ourselves.

I bring all this to mind because we are discovering our human role in a different order of magnitude. We are experiencing a disintegration of the life systems of the planet just when Earth in the diversity and resplendence of its self-expression had attained a unique grandeur. This moment deserves special attention on the part of humans who are themselves bringing about this disintegration in a manner that has never happened previously in the entire 4.6 billion years of Earth history.

We never thought of ourselves as capable of doing harm to the very structure of the planet Earth or of extinguishing the living forms that give to the planet its unique grandeur. In our efforts to reduce the planet to human control, we are, in reality, terminating the Cenozoic era, the lyric period of life development on Earth.

If such moments as dawn and dusk, birth and death, and the seasons of the year are such significant moments, how awesome, then, must be the present moment when we witness the dying of the Earth in its Cenozoic expression and the life renewal of Earth in an emerging Ecozoic era. Such reflection has a special urgency if we are ever to renew our sense of the sacred in any sphere of human activity. For we will recover our sense of wonder and our sense of the sacred only if we appreciate the universe beyond ourselves as a revelatory experience of that numinous presence whence all things come into being. Indeed, the universe is the primary sacred reality. We become sacred by our participation in this more sublime dimension of the world about us.

—"The Wild and the Sacred," in
The Great Work, 48–49

THE DETERMINING FEATURES
OF THE ECOZOIC ERA

1. Earth is a communion of subjects; it is not a collection of objects.

2. Earth exists and can survive only in its integral functioning. It cannot survive in fragments any more than any organism can survive in fragments. Yet Earth is not a global sameness. It is a differentiated unity and must be sustained in the integrity and interrelations of its many bioregional modes of expression.

3. Earth is a one-time endowment. It is subject to irreversible damage in the major patterns of its functioning.

4. The human is derivative, Earth is primary. Earth must be the primary concern of every human institution, profession, program, and activity. In economics, for instance, the first law of economics must be the preservation of the Earth economy. A rising Gross National Product with a declining Gross Earth Product reveals the absurdity of our present economy. It should be clear, such as in the medical profession, that we cannot have well people on a sick planet.

5. The entire pattern of functioning of the planet Earth is altered in the transition from the Cenozoic to the Ecozoic era. The major developments of the Cenozoic era took place entirely apart from any human intervention. In the Ecozoic era, the human will have a comprehensive influence on almost everything that happens. While the human cannot make a blade of grass, there is liable not to be a blade of grass unless it is accepted, protected, and fostered by the human. Our positive power of creativity in the natural life systems is minimal, while our power of negating is immense.

6. "Progress," to be valid, must include the entire Earth in all its component aspects. To designate human plundering of the planet as "progress" is an unbearable distortion.

7. A new role exists for both science and technology in the Ecozoic era. Science must provide a more integral understanding of the functioning of Earth and how human activity and Earth activity can be mutually enhancing. Our biological sciences especially need to develop a "feel for the organism," a greater sense of the ultimate subjectivities present in the various living beings of Earth. Our human technology must become more coherent with the technologies of the natural world.

8. New ethical principles must emerge that recognize the absolute evils of biocide and geocide, as well as the other evils concerned more directly with the human.

9. New religious sensitivities are needed, sensitivities that will recognize the sacred dimension of Earth and that will accept the natural world as the primary manifestation of the divine.

10. A new language, an Ecozoic language is needed. Our Cenozoic language is radically inadequate. A new dictionary should be compiled with new definitions of existing words and introduction of new words for the new modes of being and of functioning that are emerging.

11. Psychologically, all the archetypes of the collective unconscious attain a new validity, also new patterns of functioning; especially in our understanding of the symbols of the heroic journey, the death-rebirth symbol, the Great Mother, the tree of life.

12. New developments can be expected in ritual, in all the arts, and in literature. In drama, especially, extraordinary opportunity exists in the monumental issues that are being worked out in these times. The conflicts that

until now have been situated simply within the human are now magnified considerably through the larger contours of conflict as these emerge in this stupendous transition from the terminal Cenozoic to the emerging Ecozoic era. What we are dealing with is in epic dimensions beyond anything thus far expressed under this term.

13. Mitigation of the present ruinous situation, the recycling of materials, the diminishment of consumption, the healing of damaged ecosystems; all this will be in vain if we do these things to make the present industrial systems acceptable. They must be done, but in order to build a new order of things.

—Used by Thomas Berry for
"Remarks at the Center for Reflection
on the Second Law," Raleigh, NC

9

Moments of Grace

For Thomas Berry, "moments of grace" refers to ineffable "sacred moments of transformation" that are numinous, namely, awesome and compelling. They are irreversible and set a pattern for what comes after. Such transformative events occur at all levels of reality from the monumental collisions of galaxies to the inner workings of cellular life. For Berry, this insight provided a lens into understanding the creative tensions underlying the dynamics of the unfolding universe. The term "moments" suggests reflections on crucial events in universe evolution that determine patterns of evolutionary unfolding. Simultaneously dangerous and filled with promise, moments of grace are not bound to happen, but having done so they change everything.

This phrase—moments of grace—reveals several influences on Berry's ideas ranging from the cosmopolitan thought of the Greek Stoics, to Christian theologians, to perspectives on evolution and genetic coding. The ancient Stoics thought that a living cosmos could orient individuals and form a deep cosmopolitan citizenship that connected them to all reality. For Christian theologians, grace is a term associated with divine, providential assistance that has different interpretations. One perspective on grace is as gratuitous gift, another is that grace, once given, determines future formation, and, finally, grace as earned by personal actions.

Another influential current in moments of grace comes from those many thinkers who have grappled with Darwinian evolution. Thomas received from this evolutionary lineage a sense of dynamic change in the cosmos and an awareness of pattern that seeks to move beyond itself.

In this context, moments of grace describe those incredibly delicate interweavings of chance and necessity in evolution that need not have occurred the way they did, but having done so provide pattern for all that comes after. Such moments are the flaring forth of the universe, the coalescence of particulate matter, the springing into space of galaxies, the creative explosions of supernovae, the formation of our solar system and Earth, the emergence of life throughout the ecosphere, and many more. Such evolutionary moments of grace are coming into human awareness in the twenty-first century. Our challenge is to recognize how what has happened in the evolution of the outer world has shaped, and continues to affect, our inner world.

Understanding and responding to moments of grace is for Berry a Great Work, namely, aligning with the larger sacred purposes of the universe and the planet Earth. He was especially interested in the relationships between cultural traditions, what Berry called cultural coding, and the biological structure of life that he termed genetic coding. Berry became increasingly interested in the relationships of these codings. He pondered their alignments in human moments of grace. This occurred, as he saw it, when cultural expressions align with the spontaneities expressed in biological genetic codings. That is, genetic codings prompt humans to exist, to produce, and to propagate, and cultural codings express symbolic formations that serve to align individuals and societies with these inner drives. Awareness of these correspondences of culture and biology can bring humans into a more comprehensive participation with the cosmos.

But just as these moments of grace allure and call the human, so also they present moments of danger that transcend our rational powers. This numinous dimension of moments of grace highlight the challenge, opportunity, and potential misreading of such moments by exclusively relying on reason alone. For example, science as a way of knowing may fall short of the guidance we need. Becoming aware of the cosmic spontaneities within us requires a sensitivity that Thomas associates with the ancient healing and divining practices of the shaman. Now, he observes, we need to cultivate the shamanic dimensions of our psyche. Just as shamans among indigenous peoples evoked symbolic consciousness from their spiritual experiences of the cosmos, so also we must assemble a lived "ecology of the mind," as Gregory Bateson described in his book with that title. The special sensitivities that arise from mutually enhancing relationships with the natural world may prepare us for establishing limits and creating detachment needed for the healing of Earth. Much is given to us, according to Berry, and much is expected of us. We know the deep wonder that we are, but we also sense how detached we have become from the source of that wonder.

SACRED MOMENTS

By "moments of grace," I mean special sacred moments of transformation. The transformative experiences are the sacred experiences. We celebrate the entry into life, maturity, and the transition of death. These are sacred moments in personal life. And so in the historical process, there are these transformation moments when the future is determined in an irreversible manner. In other words, when the planet Earth came into being, that was a wonderful transformation moment that made possible everything that's happened on the planet Earth. When life came into being, it made possible everything that came afterwards. So these moments are determinative moments. And so our present is that way. What we do now, or don't do now, is going to have enormous consequences for the future: the immediate future of our own children, but the future of all generations that come after us.

—*Thomas Berry Speaks,* video by Marty Ostrow,
Finecut Productions, 2001, Transcript, p. 4

OUR MOMENT OF TRANSFORMATION

As we enter the twenty-first century, we are experiencing a moment of grace. Such moments are privileged moments. The great transformations of the universe occur at such times. The future is defined in some enduring pattern of its functioning.

There are cosmological and historical moments of grace as well as religious moments of grace. The present is one of those moments of transformation that can be considered as a cosmological, as well as a historical and a religious moment of grace.

Such a moment occurred when the star out of which our solar system was born collapsed in enormous heat, scattering itself as fragments in the vast realms of space. In the center of this star, the elements had been forming through a vast period of time until in the final heat of this explosion the hundred-some elements were present. Only then could the sun, our star, give shape to itself by gathering these fragments together with gravitational power and then leaving some nine spherical shapes sailing in elliptical paths around itself as planetary forms. At this moment, Earth too could take shape; life could be evoked; intelligence in its human form became possible.

This supernova event of a first or second generation star could be considered a cosmological moment of grace, a moment that determined the future possibilities of the solar system, Earth, and of every form of life that would ever appear on Earth.

For the more evolved multicellular organic forms of life to appear there then had to appear, the first living cell: a prokaryotic cell capable, by the energy of the sun, the carbon of the atmosphere, and the hydrogen of the sea, of a metabolic process never known previously. This original moment of transition from the nonliving to the living world, was fostered by the fierce lightning of these early times. Then, at a critical moment in the evolution of the original cell, another cell capable of using the oxygen of the atmosphere with its immense energies appeared. Photosynthesis was completed by respiration.

At this moment, the living world as we know it began to flourish until it shaped Earth anew. Daises in the meadows, the song of the mockingbird, the graceful movement of dolphins through the sea, all these became possible at this moment. We ourselves became possible. New modes of music, poetry, and painting, all these came into being in new forms against the background of the music and poetry and painting of the celestial forms circling through the heavens. . . .

Such is the context in which we must view this transition period into the twenty-first century as a moment of grace. A unique opportunity arises. For if the challenge is so absolute, the possibilities are equally comprehensive. We have identified the difficulties but also the opportunities of what is before us. A comprehensive change of consciousness is coming over the human community, especially in the industrial nations of the world. For the first time since the industrial age began, we have a profound critique of its devastation, a certain withdrawal in dismay at what is happening, along with an enticing view of the possibilities before us. . . .

Scientists are now telling the story of the universe as the epic story of evolution. We begin to understand our human identity with all the other modes of existence that constitute with us the single universe community. The one story includes us all. We are, everyone, cousins to one another. Every being is intimately present to and immediately influencing every other being.

We see quite clearly that what happens to the nonhuman happens to the human. What happens to the outer world happens to the inner world. If the outer world is diminished in its grandeur, then the emotional, imaginative, intellectual, and spiritual life of the human is diminished or extinguished. Without the soaring birds, the great forests, the sounds and coloration of the insects, the free-flowing streams, the flowering fields, the sight of the clouds by day and the stars at night, we become impoverished in all that makes us human.

There is now developing a profound mystique of the natural world. Beyond the technical comprehension of what is happening and the directions in which we need to change, we now experience the deep mysteries of existence through the wonders of the world about us. This experience has been considerably advanced through the writings of natural-history essayists. Our full entrancement with the various natural phenomena is presented with the literary skill and interpretative depth appropriate to the subject. We experience this especially in the writings of Loren Eiseley, who recovered for us in this century the full wonder of the natural world about us. He has continued the vision of the universe as this was presented to us in the nineteenth century by Ralph Waldo Emerson, Henry David Thoreau, Emily Dickinson, and John Muir.

We are now experiencing a moment of significance far beyond what any of us can imagine. What can be said is that the foundations of a new historical period, the Ecozoic era, have been established in every realm of human affairs. The mythic vision has been set into place. The distorted dream of an industrial technological paradise is being replaced by the more viable dream of a mutually enhancing human presence within an ever-renewing organic-based Earth community. The dream drives the action. In the larger cultural context, the dream becomes the myth that both guides and drives the action.

But even as we make our transition into this new century we must note that moments of grace are transient moments. The transformation must take place within a brief period. Otherwise it is gone forever. In the immense story of the universe, that so many of these dangerous moments have been navigated successfully is some indication that the universe is for us rather than against us. We need only summon these forces to our support in order to succeed. Although the human challenge to these purposes must never be underestimated, it is difficult to believe that the larger purposes of the universe or of the planet Earth will ultimately be thwarted.

—"Moments of Grace," in *The Great Work*, 196–97, 199–201

FROM CULTURAL CODING
TO GENETIC CODING

In this late twentieth century we are somewhat confused about our human situation. We need guidance. Our immediate tendency is to seek guidance from our cultural traditions, from what might be designated as our cultural coding. Yet, in this case, our need seems to be for guidance that is beyond what our cultural traditions are able to give. Our cultural traditions, it seems, are themselves a major source of our difficulty. It appears necessary that we go beyond our cultural coding, to our genetic coding, to ask for guidance.

We seldom consider going to our genetic coding for guidance in our cultural development, because we are generally unaware that our genetic coding provides the basic psychic and physical structure of our being. Our genetic coding determines not only our identity at birth; its guidance continues also in every cell of our bodies throughout the entire course of our existence, a guidance manifested through the spontaneities within us. We need only to listen to what we are being told through the very structure and functioning of our being. We do invent our cultural coding, but the power to do so is itself consequent on the imperatives of our genetic coding.

Beyond our genetic coding, we need to go to Earth, as the source whence we came, and ask for its guidance, for Earth carries the psychic structure, as well as the physical form of every living being upon the planet. Our confusion is not only within ourselves; it concerns also our role in the planetary community. Even beyond Earth, we need to go to the universe and inquire concerning the basic issues of reality and value, for, even more than Earth, the universe carries the deep mysteries of our existence within itself.

We cannot discover ourselves without first discovering the universe, Earth, and the imperatives of our own being. Each of these has a creative power and a vision far beyond any rational thought or cultural creation of which we are capable. Nor should we think of these as isolated from our own individual being or from the human community. We have no existence except within Earth and within the universe.

The human is less a being on Earth or in the universe than a dimension of Earth and indeed of the universe itself. The shaping of our human mode of being depends on the support and guidance of this comprehensive order of things. We are an immediate concern of every other being in the universe. Ultimately, our guidance on any significant issue must emerge from this comprehensive source.

Nor is this source distant from us. The universe is so immediate to us, is such an intimate presence, that it escapes our notice, yet whatever authenticity exists in our cultural creations is derived from these spontaneities within us, spontaneities that come from an abyss of energy and a capacity for intelligible order of which we have only the faintest glimmer in our conscious awareness. . . .

In moments of confusion such as the present, we are not left simply to our own rational contrivances. We are supported by the ultimate powers of the universe as they make themselves present to us through the spontaneities within our own beings. We need only become sensitized to these spontaneities, not with a naive simplicity, but with critical appreciation. This intimacy with our genetic endowment, and through this endowment with the larger cosmic process, is not primarily the role of the philosopher, priest, prophet, or professor. It is the role of the shamanic personality, a type that is emerging once again in our society.

More than any other of the human types concerned with the sacred, the shamanic personality journeys into the far regions of the cosmic mystery and brings back the vision and the power needed by the human community at the most elementary level. The shamanic personality speaks and best understands the language of the various creatures of Earth. Not only is the shamanic type emerging in our society, but also the shamanic dimension of the psyche itself. In periods of significant cultural creativity, this aspect of the psyche takes on a pervasive role throughout the society and shows up in all the basic institutions and professions. The great scientists do their best work through this dimension of the psyche.

This shamanic insight is especially important just now, when history is being made not primarily within nations or between nations, but between humans and Earth, with all its living creatures. In this context all our professions and institutions must be judged primarily by the extent to which they foster this mutually enhancing human-Earth relationship.

If the supreme disaster in the comprehensive story of Earth is our present closing down of the major life systems of the planet, then the supreme need of our times is to bring about a healing of Earth through this mutually enhancing human presence to the Earth community. To achieve this mode of presence, a new type of sensitivity is needed, a sensitivity that is something more than romantic attachment to some of the more brilliant manifestations of the natural world, a sensitivity that comprehends the larger patterns of nature, its severe demands as well as its delightful aspects, and is willing to see the human diminish so that other life forms might flourish.

These sensitivities are beginning to emerge throughout the human community in the multitude of activities that can generally be indicated under the general title of ecological movements. Ecology can rightly be considered the supreme subversive science. In responding to the external situation and to the imperatives of our own nature, these ecological movements are threatening all those cultural commitments that have brought about the present devastation of Earth. This rising conflict is beginning to dominate every aspect of the human process.

—"The Dream of the Earth: Our Way into the Future,"
in *The Dream of the Earth*, 194–95, 211–12

THE WONDER OF EARTH

As we enter the twenty-first century we observe a widespread awakening to the wonder of Earth. This we can observe in the writings of naturalists and the environmental organizations dedicated to preserving the integrity of the planet. There are also those in the scientific world who give expression to the wonder of things, such as Peter Raven, Norman Myers, Lynn Margulis, Eric Chaisson, Ursula Goodenough, Brian Swimme, and others who are revealing to us the larger pattern as well as the intricate details of the visible world about us.

The human venture depends absolutely on this quality of awe and reverence and joy in Earth and all that lives and grows upon Earth. As soon as we isolate ourselves from these currents of life and from the profound mood that these engender within us, then our basic life-satisfactions are diminished. None of our machine-made products, none of our computer-based achievements can evoke that total commitment to life from the subconscious regions of our being that is needed to sustain Earth and carry both ourselves and the integral Earth community into the hazardous future.

How we feel about ourselves and about the Earth process are questions of utmost urgency, especially when we are presented with the notion of Earth as a collection of commodities to be bought and sold. The very meaning of Earth is involved in this question, as are the human energies needed to assist in shaping a desirable future. In our quest for understanding, we might begin with the observation that Earth is the manifestation of a vast amount of energy caught up in a diversity of designs for which there is no accounting in terms of human understanding or imagination. In a sequence of mutations, great stores of energy were deposited within Earth, not only as fossil fuels but also as life forces within the very structure of matter.

Our present peril is not the first that Earth and living things upon it have endured. Earth found its way into being amid an amazing sequence of both creative and destructive experiences. A long sequence of cataclysmic events has shaped the continents and the various forms of life that have themselves engaged in a continuing struggle for survival. But the present danger to the planet is the first conscious intrusion on this scale into the natural rhythms of the Earth process. This is something radically different from the seismic convulsions, the glacial advances, the earlier emergence and disappearance of species. It is the exploitation of energies in a definitive form. It is a turn from the storing of energies to the burning off of energies in a manner and in a volume such that they cannot be replaced in any conceivable period of human historical existence. Because of our need to fuel the industrial world, we have created a technosphere incompatible with the biosphere. . . .

We must feel that we are supported by that same power that brought Earth into being, that power that spun the galaxies into space that lit the sun and brought the moon into its orbit. That is the power by which living forms grew up out of Earth and came to a special mode of reflexive consciousness in the human. This is the force that brought us through more than a million years of wandering as hunters and gatherers; this is that same vitality that led to the establishment of our cities and inspired the thinkers, artists, and poets of the ages. Those same forces are still present; indeed, we might feel their impact at this time and understand that we are not isolated in the chill of space with the burden of the future upon us and without the aid of any other power.

We are a pervasive presence. By definition we are that reality in whom the entire planet Earth comes to a special mode of reflexive consciousness. We are ourselves a mystical quality of Earth, a unifying principle, an integration of the various polarities of the material and the spiritual, the physical and the psychic, the natural and the artistic, the intuitive and the scientific. We are the unity in which all these inhere and achieve a special mode of functioning. In this way the human acts as a pervading logos. If the human is microcosmos, the cosmos is macroanthropos. We are each the cosmic person, the *Mahapurusha*, the Great Person of Hinduism, expressed in the universe itself.

This being so, there is need to be sensitive to Earth, for the destiny of Earth identifies with our own destiny, exploitation of Earth is exploitation of the human, elimination of the aesthetic splendors of Earth is the diminishment of existence. We do not serve the human by blasting the mountains apart for mineral resources, for in losing the wonder and awesome qualities of the mountains we destroy an urgent dimension of our own reality.

Ancient rituals through which we communicated with Earth and fostered its productivity may no longer seem fully effective. Yet they do express a profound respect for the mystery of Earth. It would be philosophically unrealistic, historically inaccurate, and scientifically unwarranted to say that the human and Earth no longer have an intimate and reciprocal emotional relationship.

We are not lacking in the dynamic forces needed to create the future. We live immersed in a sea of energy beyond all comprehension. But this energy, in an ultimate sense, is ours not by domination but by invocation.

—"The Dynamics of the Future," in
The Great Work, 166–67, 174–75

FOURFOLD WISDOM

In these opening years of the twenty-first century, as the human community experiences a rather difficult situation in its relation with the natural world, we might reflect that a fourfold wisdom is available to guide us into the future: the wisdom of indigenous peoples, the wisdom of women, the wisdom of the classical traditions, and the wisdom of science. We need to consider these wisdom traditions in terms of their distinctive functioning, in the historical periods of their fluorescence, and in their common support for the emerging age when humans will be a mutually enhancing presence on Earth.

It becomes increasingly evident that in our present situation that no one of these traditions is sufficient. We need all of the traditions. Each has its own distinctive achievements, limitations distortions, its own special contribution toward an integral wisdom tradition that seems to be taking shape in the emerging twenty-first century. Each of the traditional modes of understanding seems to be experiencing a renewal. For the first time the indigenous traditions are accepted as setting the basic model for human presence to the universe. . . . The Forum on Religion and Ecology at Yale, which grew out of a three-year series of conferences at Harvard on the world religions and their views of nature, is an important new direction for examining the wisdom of the religious traditions for guidance into the next century.

For the first time also, we begin to understand that the human project belongs in the care and under the direction of both women and men. This was a movement out of a patriarchal society into a truly integral human order. So too the traditional Western civilization must withdraw from its efforts at dominion over Earth. This will be one of the most severe disciplines in the future, for the Western addiction to economic dominance is even more powerful than the drive toward political dominance.

Then, finally, there is the epic of evolution, the contribution of science toward the future. The universe story is our story, individually and as the human community. In this context we can feel secure in our efforts to fulfill the Great Work before us. The guidance, the inspiration and the energy we need is available. The accomplishment of the Great Work is the task not simply of the human community but of the entire planet Earth. Even beyond Earth, it is the Great Work of the universe itself.

—"The Fourfold Wisdom," in
The Great Work, 176, 194–95

THE ECOLOGICAL AGE

Presently, we are entering another historical period, one that might be designated as the ecological age. I use the term *ecological* in its primary meaning as the relation of an organism to its environment, but also as an indication of the interdependence of all the living and nonliving systems of Earth. This vision of a planet integral with itself throughout its spatial extent and its evolutionary sequence is of primary importance if we are to have the psychic power to undergo the psychic and social transformations that are being demanded of us. These transformations require the assistance of the entire planet, not merely the forces available to the human. Otherwise we mistake the order of magnitude in this challenge. It is not simply adaptation to a reduced supply of fuels or to some modification in our system of social or economic controls. Nor is it some slight change in our educational system. What is happening is something of a far greater magnitude. It is a radical change in our mode of consciousness. Our challenge is to create a new language, even a new sense of what it is to be human. It is to transcend not only national limitations, but even our species isolation, to enter into the larger community of living species. This brings about a completely new sense of reality and of value.

"The Ecological Age," in
The Dream of the Earth, 41–42

10

The Role of the Human

Thomas Berry sought to evoke a depth of energies whereby the human might bring forward the flourishing of the Earth community. He saw that this will require a reinterpretation of our role as something more than consumers of goods or exploiters of resources. Berry invites us to find our role within the dynamic forces of nature that have given birth to living things and continue to provide sustenance for our life. This helps us to see ourselves beyond our role in family or society or politics or church. Rather it calls us into our role as a cosmological being, one that completes the powers of the universe and Earth. Such a calling is at the heart of religious traditions and has inspired sages and teachers throughout the last several millennia. Now, however, the task is to place ourselves within the context of deep time—a fourteen-billion-year evolving history in which we are late arrivals. If it took Earth a billion years to bring forth the first cell and another several billion to give rise to multicellular creatures and finally see the emergence of life on land and sea, on mountain tops and in the depths of the oceans—what is our role as homo sapiens? Within the vast sweep of our planetary history of 4.6 billion years, we are a mere two hundred thousand years old. What does this mean for us to become not merely self-reflective mammals but mammals with wisdom—inherited and cultivated anew.

Berry suggests the urgency of this task is upon us with the closing down of a geological era of some sixty-five million years, the Cenozoic era. He observes that we have a Great Work now to lay down the foundations for the Ecozoic era. This will involve such projects as creating sustainable communities based on renewable energy and green industries, organic agriculture and food systems, livable cities and clean transportation. All of this was part of his concern as he frequently identified people working in these areas like John and Nancy Todd and Amory Lovins in energy, Wes Jackson and Wendell Berry in agriculture and food, David Orr in green buildings.

All of these individuals are participating in what he would call the Great Work. Indeed, everyone has a part to play in this transformation. He would often reflect on how we do not choose when we are born or into what culture or circumstances. However, he observed that "the ability of our lives depends on the manner in which we come to understand and fulfill our assigned role." To undertake such a Great Work requires that we share our dreams for a life-sustaining future. Berry calls this our "shared dream experience" which evokes spontaneous and creative energies at the heart of universe emergence.

But there is still more. The challenge of our times is not simply toward a sustainable future, but rather one that provides the conditions for flourishing of both people and planet. For this he lays down the ultimate challenge, namely, "reinventing the human." We have become an unviable species, one that can image for the first time its own demise. This is not simply witnessing the extinction of other species, but calling into question our own longevity—our own future prospects. This is a radical shift in human consciousness—one that will require a depth of creativity and strength still not yet fully understood or imagined. This is what lies ahead in the years to come. We are finding our way forward supported by the powers of the universe and Earth in a moment of both destruction and renewal.

THE GREAT WORK

History is governed by those overarching movements that give shape and meaning to life by relating the human venture to the larger destinies of the universe. Creating such a movement might be called the Great Work of a people. There have been Great Works in the past: the Great Work of the classical Greek world with its understanding of the human mind and creation of the Western humanist traditions; the Great Work of Israel in articulating a new experience of the divine in human affairs; the Great Work of Rome in gathering the peoples of the Mediterranean world and of Western Europe into an ordered relation with one another. So too in the medieval period there was the task of giving a first shape to the Western world in its Christian form. The symbols of this Great Work were medieval cathedrals rising so graciously into the heavens from the region of the Frankish empire. There the divine and the human could be present to each other in some grand manner.

In India, the Great Work was to lead human thought into spiritual experiences of time and eternity and their mutual presence to each other with a unique subtlety of expression. China created one of the most elegant and most human civilizations we have ever known as its Great Work. In America, the Great Work of the First Peoples was to occupy this continent and establish an intimate rapport with the powers that brought this continent into existence in all its magnificence. They did this through their ceremonies such as . . . the sweat lodge and the vision quest of the Plains Indians, through the Chantways of the Dineh/Navaho and the Katsina rituals of the Hopi. Through these and a multitude of other aspects of the indigenous cultures of this continent, certain models were established of how humans became integral with the larger context of our existence here on the planet Earth.

While all of these efforts at fulfilling a Great Work have made significant contributions to the human venture, they were all limited in their fulfillment and bear the marks of their deeply human flaws and imperfections. Here in North America it is with a poignant feeling and foreboding concerning the future that we begin to realize that the European occupation of this continent, however admirable its intentions, has been flawed from the beginning in its assault on the indigenous peoples and its plundering of the land. Its most impressive achievements were establishing for the settlers a sense of personal rights, participatory governance, and religious freedom.

If there was also advancement of scientific insight and technological skills leading to relief from many of the ills and poverty of the European peoples, this advancement was accompanied by devastation of this continent in its natural florescence by the suppression of the way of life of its indigenous peoples and by communicating to them many previously unknown diseases, such as smallpox, tuberculosis, diphtheria, and measles. Although Europeans had developed a certain immunity to these diseases, they were consistently fatal to Indians, who had never known such diseases and had developed no immunities.

Meanwhile, the incoming Europeans committed themselves to development of the new industrial age that was beginning to dominate human consciousness. New achievements in science, technology, industry, commerce, and finance had indeed brought the human community into a new age. Yet those who brought this new historical period into being saw only the bright side of these achievements. They had little comprehension of the devastation they were causing on this continent and throughout the planet, a devastation that finally led to an impasse in our relations with the natural world. Our commercial-industrial obsessions have disturbed the biosystems of this continent in a depth never known previously in the historical course of human affairs.

The Great Work now, as we move into a new millennium, is to carry out the transition from a period of human devastation of Earth to a period when humans would be present to the planet in a mutually beneficial manner. This historical change is something more than the transition from the classical Roman period to the medieval period, or from the medieval period to modern times. Such a transition has no historical parallel since the geobiological transition that took place sixty-five million years ago, when the period of the dinosaurs was terminated and a new biological age begun. So now we awaken to a period of extensive disarray in the biological structure and functioning of the planet. . . .

Now, in these closing years of the twentieth century, we find a growing concern for our responsibility to the generations who will live in the twenty-first century.

Perhaps the most valuable heritage we can provide for future generations is some sense of the Great Work that is before them of moving the human project from its devastating exploitation to a benign presence. We need to give them some indication of how the next generation can fulfill this work in an effective manner. For the success or failure of any historical age is the extent to which those living at that time have fulfilled the special role that history has imposed upon them. No age lives completely unto itself. Each age has only what it receives from the prior generation. Just now we have abundant evidence that the various species of life, the mountains and rivers, and even the vast ocean itself, which once we thought beyond serious impact from humans, will survive only in their damaged integrity.

The Great Work before us, the task of moving modern industrial civilization from its present devastating influence on Earth to a more benign mode of presence, is not a role that we have chosen. It is a role given to us, beyond any consultation with ourselves. We did not choose. We were chosen by some power beyond ourselves for this historical task. We do not choose the moment of our birth, who our parents will be, our particular culture or the historical moment when we will be born. We do not choose the status of spiritual insight or political or economic conditions that will be the context of our lives. We are, as it were, thrown into existence with a challenge and a role that is beyond any personal choice. The nobility of our lives, however, depends upon the manner in which we come to understand and fulfill our assigned role.

Yet, we must believe that those powers that assign our role must in that same act bestow upon us the ability to fulfill this role. We must believe that we are cared for and guided by these same powers that bring us into being.

Our own special role, which we will hand on to our children, is that of managing the arduous transition from the terminal Cenozoic to the emerging Ecozoic era, the period when humans will be present to the planet as participating members of the comprehensive Earth community. . . .

We might observe here that the Great Work of a people is the work of all the people. No one is exempt. Each of us has our individual life pattern and responsibilities. Yet beyond these concerns, each person in and through their personal work assists in the Great Work. Personal work needs to be aligned with the Great Work. This can be seen in the medieval period as the basic patterns of personal life and craft skills were aligned within the larger work of the civilizational effort. While this alignment is more difficult in these times it must remain an ideal to be sought.

We cannot doubt that we too have been given the intellectual vision, the spiritual insight, and even the physical resources we need for carrying out the transition that is demanded of these times, transition from the period when humans were a disruptive force on the planet Earth to the period when humans become present to the planet in a manner that is mutually enhancing.

—"The Great Work," in
The Great Work, 1–3, 7–8, 10–11

REINVENTING THE HUMAN
AT THE SPECIES LEVEL

The present human situation can be described in three sentences:

1. In the twentieth century the glory of the human has become the desolation of Earth.

2. The desolation of Earth is becoming the destiny of the human.

3. All human institutions, professions, programs, and activities must now be judged primarily by the extent to which they inhibit, ignore, or foster a mutually enhancing human-Earth relationship.

In the light of these statements, it is proposed that the historical mission of our times is:

◆ To reinvent the human

◆ At the species level

◆ With critical reflection

◆ Within the community of life systems

◆ In a time-developmental context

◆ By means of story and

◆ Shared dream experience.

The first phase, "To reinvent the human," suggests that the planetary crisis we are facing seems to be beyond the competence of our present cultural traditions. What is needed is something beyond existing traditions to bring us back to the most fundamental aspect of the human: giving shape to ourselves. The issue has never been as critical as it is now. The human is at an impasse because we have brought the entire set of life systems of the planet to an impasse. The viability of the human is in question.

Our present difficulty is that we envisage the universe simply in its physical dimensions. We have lost the awareness that the universe has from the beginning been a psychic-spiritual as well as material-physical reality. It has taken the entire course of the evolutionary process for the universe to find its expression in the florescence of living forms and in the various modes of consciousness that are manifested throughout Earth.

The immense curvature of space holds all things together in an embrace that is sufficiently closed to provide structural integrity to the universe and yet sufficiently open to enable the universe to continue its unfolding. Within this context we need a new appreciation of our cosmocentric identity.

Second, we must work "at the species level" because our problems are primarily problems of species. This is clear in every aspect of the human. As regards economics, we need not simply a national or a global economy, but a species economy. Our schools of business teach the skills whereby the greatest possible amount of natural resources is processed as quickly as possible, put through the consumer economy, and then passed on to the junk heap where it is at best useless and at worst toxic to every living being. There is need for the human species to develop reciprocal economic relationships with other life forms, providing a sustaining pattern of mutual support, as is the case with other life systems.

As regards law, we need a special legal tradition that would provide for the legal rights of geological and biological, as well as human, components of the Earth community. A legal system exclusively for humans is not realistic. Habitat, for example, must be given legal status as sacred and inviolable.

Third, I say "with critical reflection" because this reinventing of the human needs to be done with the utmost competence. We need all our scientific knowledge. We cannot abandon our technologies. We must, however, ensure that our technologies are coherent with the technologies of the natural world. Our knowledge needs to be a creative response to the natural world rather than a domination of the natural world.

We insist on critical understanding as we enter the Ecological age in order to avoid a romantic attraction to the natural world that would not meet the urgencies of what we are about. The natural world is violent and dangerous as well as serene and benign. Our intimacies with the natural world must not conceal the fact that we are engaged in a constant struggle with natural forces. Life has a bitter and burdensome aspect at all levels, yet its total effect is to strengthen the inner substance of the living world and to provide the never-ending excitement of a grand adventure.

Fourth, we need to reinvent the human "within the community of life systems." Because Earth is not adequately understood either by our spiritual or by our scientific traditions, the human has become an addendum or an intrusion. We have found this situation to our liking since it enables us to avoid the problem of integral presence to Earth. This attitude prevents us from considering Earth as a single society with ethical relations determined primarily by the well-being of the total Earth community.

But while Earth is a single integral community, it is not a global sameness. It is highly differentiated in bioregional communities—in Arctic as well as tropical regions, in mountains, valleys, plains and coastal regions. These bioregions can be described as identifiable geographical areas of interacting life systems that are relatively self-sustaining in the ever-renewing processes of nature. As the functional units of the planet, these bioregions can be described as self-propagating, self-nourishing, self-educating, self-governing, self-healing, and self-fulfilling communities.

Human population levels, our economic activities, our educational processes, our governance, our healing, our fulfillment must be envisaged as integral with this community process. Earth itself is the primary progenitor, economist, educator, lawgiver, healer, and fulfillment for everything on Earth.

There are great difficulties in identifying just how to establish a viable context for a flourishing and sustainable human mode of being. Of one thing we can be sure, however, and it is that our own future is inseparable from the future of the larger life community. That is because this life community brought us into being and sustains us in every expression of our human quality of life—in our aesthetic and emotional sensitivities, our intellectual perceptions, our sense of the divine, and our physical nourishment and bodily healing.

Fifth, reinventing the human must take place in "a time developmental context." This constitutes what might be called the cosmological dimension of the program we are outlining here. Our sense of who we are and what our role is must begin where the universe begins. Not only the formation of the universe but also our own physical and spiritual shaping begin with the origin of the universe.

—Appendix in *The Christian Future*
and the Fate of Earth, 117–20

DIFFERENTIATION, SUBJECTIVITY, AND COMMUNION

The ethical formation required is governed by three basic principles: differentiation, subjectivity, and communion.

Our present course is a violation of each of these three principles in their most primordial expression. Whereas the basic direction of the evolutionary process is toward constant differentiation within a functional order of things, our modern world is directed toward monocultures. This is the inherent direction of the entire industrial age. Industry requires a standardization, an invariant process of multiplication with no enrichment of meaning. In an acceptable cultural context, we would recognize that the unique properties of each reality determine its absolute value both for the individual and for the community. These are fulfilled in each other. Violation of the individual is an assault on the community.

As a second ethical imperative derived from the cosmological process, we find that each individual is not only different from every other being in the universe but also has its own inner articulation. Each being in its subjective depths carries the numinous mystery whence the universe emerges into being. This we might identify as the sacred depth of the individual, one's subjectivity.

The third ethical imperative of communion reminds us that the entire universe is bonded together in such a way that the presence of each individual is felt throughout the entire spatial and temporal range of the universe. This capacity for bonding of the components of the universe with each other enables the vast variety of beings to come into existence in that gorgeous profusion that we observe about us.

—Appendix in *The Christian Future*
and the Fate of Earth, 120–21

THE STORY OF THE UNIVERSE

From this we can appreciate the directing and energizing role played by "the story of the universe." This story that we know through empirical observation of the world is our most valuable resource in establishing a viable mode of being for the human species, as well as for all those stupendous life systems whereby Earth achieves its grandeur, its fertility, and its capacity for endless self-renewal.

This story, as told in its galactic expansion, its Earth formation, its life emergence, and its manifestation of consciousness in the human, fulfills in our times the role of the mythic accounts of the universe that existed in earlier times when human awareness was dominated by a spatial mode of consciousness. The story represents a transition in human awareness from the universe as cosmos to the universe as cosmogenesis. It represents a shift in the spiritual path from a mandala-like journey to the center of an abiding world to the great irreversible journey of the universe itself as the primary sacred journey. This journey of the universe is the journey of each individual being in the universe. So this story of the great journey is an exciting revelatory story that gives us our macrophase identity—the larger dimension of meaning that we need. To be able to identify the microphase of our being with the macrophase mode of the universe is the quintessence of what needs to be achieved.

The present imperative of the human is that this journey continue on into the future in the integrity of the unfolding life systems of Earth, which presently are threatened in their survival. Our great failure is the termination of the journey for so many of the most brilliant species of the life community. The horrendous fact is that we are, as the scientist Norman Myers has indicated, in an extinction spasm that is likely to produce "the greatest single setback to life's abundance and diversity since the first flickerings of life almost four billion years ago."[1] The labor and care expanded over some billions of years and untold billions of experiments to bring forth such a gorgeous Earth is being negated within less than a century for what is considered "progress" toward a better life in a better world.

—Appendix in *The Christian Future and The Fate of Earth* 121–22

SHARED DREAM EXPERIENCE

The final aspect of our statement concerning the ethical imperative of our times is "the shared dream experience." The creative process, whether in the human or the cosmological order, is too mysterious for easy explanation. Yet, we all have the experience of creative activity. Since human processes involve much trial and error, with only occasional success at any high level of distinction, we may well believe that the cosmological process has also passed through a vast period of experimentation in order to achieve the ordered processes of our present universe.

In both instances, something is perceived in a dim and uncertain manner, something radiant with meaning that draws us on to a further clarification of our understanding and our activity. Suddenly, out of the formless condition, a formed reality appears. This process can be described in many ways, as a groping, or as a feeling, or as an imaginative process. The most appropriate way of describing the process seems to be that of dream realization. The universe appears to be the fulfillment of something so highly imaginative and so overwhelming that it must have been dreamed into existence.

But if the dream is creative we must also recognize that few things are so destructive as a dream or entrancement that has lost the integrity of its meaning and entered into exaggerated and destructive manifestation. This has happened often enough with political ideologies and with religious visionaries, but there is no dream or entrancement in the history of Earth that has wrought the destruction that is taking place in the entrancement with industrial civilization. Such entrancement must be considered as a profound cultural pathology. It can be dealt with only by a correspondingly deep cultural therapy.

Such is our present situation. We are involved not simply with an ethical issue but with a disturbance sanctioned by the very structures of the culture itself in its present phase. The governing dream of the twentieth century appears as a kind of ultimate manifestation of that deep inner rage of Western society against its earthly condition. As with the goose that laid the golden egg, so planet Earth is assaulted in a vain effort to possess not simply the magnificent fruits of the earth, but the power itself whereby these splendors have emerged.

At such a moment, a new revelatory experience is needed, an experience wherein human consciousness awakens to the grandeur and sacred quality of Earth process. This awakening is our human participation in the dream of Earth, the dream that is carried in its integrity not in any of Earth's cultural expressions but in the depths of our genetic coding. Therein Earth functions at a depth beyond our capacity for active thought. We can only be sensitized to what is being revealed to us. Such participation in the dream of Earth we probably have not had since earlier times, but therein lies our hope for the future of ourselves and for the entire Earth community.

—"Reinventing the Human at the Species Level," in Appendix
to *The Christian Future and the Fate of Earth*, 122–23

11

Alienation and Renewal

Thomas Berry was deeply affected by the movement of existentialism arising in post-war Europe. At this time, the writings and novels of Jean-Paul Sartre and Albert Camus were being widely read. The collapse of meaning after two World Wars led to a profound sense of alienation of humans from one another and from the world around them. Berry's understanding of the roots of this separation gave him great empathy for human loneliness and suffering. In addition, he had a keen interest in the alternative cultural and political movements that arose in the 1960s in response to this alienation. His engagement with the 1960s generation was evident, not only in his teaching, but also in his concern for the struggles of students. It would not be unusual to find Berry with a group of students at the Broadway Diner in Riverdale discussing meaning and alienation over coffee and a grilled cheese sandwich.

Berry was profoundly aware of estrangement as a pervasive dimension of modern life. He noted the depth of human separation from one another, especially between the affluent and the impoverished. He especially observed the distancing we have experienced from nature and the inevitable destruction this has caused.

His suggested antidote for these multiforms of alienation is an understanding of the bonded relationality of the universe and Earth, which has birthed us and nurtures us still. By recovering this relationality, we can begin a process, of healing by renewal and restoration. Berry realized that we need humility in this process because humans can't give life. "We can only accept, defend, foster, and occasionally assist in healing the work of the living."

In addition to alienation, Berry understood that loneliness surrounds humans, especially when they see themselves as apart from nature and not part of the Earth community. His essay "Loneliness and Presence" is from a paper he delivered at a Harvard conference on Religion and Animals in 1999. There he moved the audience with his powerful recognition that the universe is not a collection of objects, but a communion of subjects. Indeed, this phrase "a communion of subjects" became the title of the book from the conference.

In this paper he touched the audience of scholars of both science and religion with his unique articulation of "mutual indwelling." Here he observed how the living and nonliving world have an inner principle of being. This is why we sense reciprocity with animals, fish, and birds. It is also why we can sense a spirit of a place—one's homeland or the heartland, a special wilderness or woodland, open fields or meadows, rivers and mountains. This is no doubt why we seek renewal and re-creation in nature. The sense of deep resonance with nature is widespread and enduring among humans. This is what Ed Wilson and Stephen Kellert have called "biophilia."

While we may have lost this capacity in the modern world, it is resurfacing in such experiences as people trying to rescue beached whales, or protect elephants, or assist nesting turtles, or preserve habitats for migrating birds and butterflies. This pressing desire to go beyond alienation and loneliness so as to be in the presence of living creature is one of our greatest sources of hope. For such experiences of presence ignite in us a feeling of belonging to something larger—to the great dance of life that flows through us and connects us to a vast mystery that holds us all together.

DISCOVERING OUR PLACE

Alienation is, in some sense, the oldest and most universal human experience. It is our human condition: the difficulty of discovering our personal identity and our proper place in the universe. Particularly in Western civilization in the nineteenth and twentieth centuries, humans have experienced the challenge of authentic existence while moving through a series of rapid historical transformations. Alienation of the workman from the means and benefits of his production was the central social issue from the 1848 manifesto of Karl Marx (1818–1883) until the dissolution of the Soviet regime in 1991. Alienation of the "authentic self" from the "false self" that we adopt has been a central issue in psychotherapy throughout the twentieth century. Alienation was especially severe in the counter-cultural movements of the radical left in America in the 1960s, both its dramatic protests against existing social structures and the "flower people" of that period, with their romantic-mystical rebellion against the harshness of industrial life.

In the opening years of the twenty-first century, we are experiencing a new alienation in our inability to relate effectively to the integral functioning of Earth. This alienation, which results from an extreme anthropocentrism and dedication to consumerism, is causing the exploitation and devastation of the planet, supposedly for human advantage. Until recently, few people have realized the extent to which human fulfillment depends on the integral functioning of Earth in all the grandeur of its natural landscapes—the forests, mountains, woodlands, rivers, and lakes—and the wonder of its wildlife: animals, insects, fish, and songbirds.

Alienation from the world of nature has led us to extravagant expectations concerning the benefits of our modern technologies. These expectations have blinded us to the evils inherent in the very solutions to life's difficulties we were proposing. By using chemical fertilizers, we increased our grain harvest but destroyed the natural fertility of the soil. Because of our clear-cut assault on the woodlands, the forests can no longer renew themselves. In relentlessly pursuing marine life, we depleted the abundance that was there for millennia.

In the last two centuries, as we have become more proficient in manipulating the nonhuman components of the Earth community, we have become progressively alienated from the most elementary awareness of our role and place in that community. We expected the entire universe to respond to us, the human component, as the ultimate reference and arbiter of value. Frustrated when we realize that we do not have control over the world around us, we sink into a deepening cultural impasse.

In becoming a commerce-dependent consumer society, we have ignored the essential elements and ideals necessary to sustain any viable human community. For example, by enclosing ourselves in automobiles, we have isolated people from one another and destroyed a certain sense of community. Moreover, we find that the distance between the affluent and the less well-off and from the impoverished is constantly increasing. We are isolated and alienated, both as individuals and as communities. We are held together mainly by the political-legal binding of the modern nationalist state and by our dependence on an industrial, commercial, and consumer society. . . .

It takes a universe to bring humans into being, a universe to educate humans, a universe to fulfill the human mode of being. More immediately, it takes a solar system and a planet Earth to shape, educate, and fulfill the human. The difficulty in recent times is that the concern of the human in all the various traditions, with few exceptions, has been focused almost exclusively on interhuman and divine-human relations. Human-Earth relations have not been given the comprehensive consideration needed. That is where our contemporary challenge is located.

—"Alienation," in *The Sacred Universe*, 35–36, 44

BONDED RELATIONSHIPS

In our modern empirical inquiry into the origin and structure of the universe, we have attained a new understanding of the universe as the ultimate referent of every mode of being. Indeed, science loses its validity if this bonded relationship of every mode of being in the universe to every other mode of being is not accepted. We can explain nothing if we cannot explain the whole. Our explanation of any part of the universe is integral to our understanding of the universe itself.

It is most significant for humans to experience themselves as brought into being, sustained in being, and fulfilled through the comprehensive universe. This coming forth from a physical and nurturing source requires also our return to the universe as our final destiny. In more proximate terms, whatever is said of the universe applies proportionately to Earth context. The various components of the Earth form a single integral community.

In this manner, our alienation is definitively overcome within a unified understanding of ourselves, of the universe, and all the forces present therein. The genius of our times is to join the physical identification, experience and understanding of Earth, given by scientific inquiry, with the traditional mythic symbols and rituals associated with the Great Mother Earth. To appreciate both of these in their proper relationship is to overcome our alienation from the universe and from Earth. This understanding should evoke the emotional and imaginative sympathies needed for the sensitive care humans need to give to the natural world and also provide for our aesthetic excitement and celebration of the natural world. —"Alienation," in *The Sacred Universe*, 45–46

RENEWAL

Yet we must think about and respond to the urgency of a renewal of the integral community of life systems throughout Earth. Renewal is a community project. Only the community survives; nothing survives as an individual. Here our sciences reach their limits, both in understanding and in efficacy. The shallow regions of control that humans possess over the natural life systems are vast in their powers of devastation, but pathetically limited in their powers of renewal. We can take away, but we cannot give life. We can only accept, defend, foster, and occasionally assist in healing the world of the living. The skill to carry out these four functions will be the great skill of the future. Our hope is that the vital forces within the diminished life systems of Earth can themselves renew, at least in part, the creativity shown over the centuries. For example, we see the system's creativity at Krakatoa, the island between Sumatra and Java, whose life systems were almost completely destroyed by a volcanic explosion in 1883, and then with marvelous recuperative powers returned to life. This resurgence occurred independently of any human assistance.

To bring about renewal on the larger continents, where human presence and the industrial process have exhausted the land and fouled the air, polluted the rivers and ruined the forests, and to restore the great shoals of fish that once filled the seas: this is the challenge. We need to understand death-renewal symbolism with new depth. What is needed is a new pattern of rapport with the planet. Here we come to the critical transformation needed in the emotional, aesthetic, spiritual, and religious orders of life. Only a change that profound in human consciousness can remedy the deep cultural pathology manifest in such destructive behavior. Such a change is not possible, however, so long as we fail to appreciate the planet that provides us with a world abundant in the volume and variety of food for our nourishment, a world exquisite in supplying beauty of form, sweetness of taste, delicate fragrances for our enjoyment, and exciting challenges for us to overcome with skill and action. The poets and artists can help restore this sense of rapport with the natural world. It is this renewed energy of reciprocity with nature, in all of its complexity and remarkable beauty, that can help provide the psychic and spiritual energies necessary for the work ahead.

—"Alienation," in *The Sacred Universe*, 47–48

LONELINESS AND PRESENCE

At the time of his treaty with the European settlers in 1854, Chief Seattle of the Squamish tribe along the North Pacific coast is reported to have said that when the last animals will have perished, "humans would die of loneliness." This was an insight that might never have occurred to a European settler. Yet this need for more-than-human companionship has a significance and an urgency that we have begun to appreciate in more recent times. To understand this primordial need that humans have for the natural world and its animal inhabitants, we might reflect on the needs of our children, the two-, three-, and four-year-olds especially. We can hardly communicate with them in any meaningful way except through pictures and stories of humans and animals and fields and trees, of flowers, birds, and butterflies, of sea and sky. These present to the child a world of wonder and beauty and intimacy, a world sufficiently enticing to enable the child to overcome the sorrows they necessarily experience from their earliest years. This is the world that we all grow up in, to some extent in the reality of it, to some extent through pictures and stories.

The child experiences that "friendship relation" that exists among all things throughout the universe, the universe Thomas Aquinas speaks of in his commentary on the writings of Pseudo-Dionysius the Areopagite, the mystical Christian Neoplatonist of the late fifth century. Indeed, we cannot be truly ourselves in any adequate manner without all our companion beings throughout Earth. This larger community constitutes our great self. Even beyond Earth, we have an intimate presence to the universe in its comprehensive reality. The scientists' quest for their greater selves is what prompts their relentless drive toward an ever-greater understanding of the world around them.

Our intimacy with the universe demands an alternative presence to the smallest particles, as well as to the vast range of stars splashed across the skies in every direction. More immediately present to our consciousness here on Earth are the landscape; the sky above, the earth below; the grasses, the flowers, the forests, and the fauna present themselves to our opening senses. Each in its own distinctive perfection fills our mind, our imagination, our emotional attraction.

Of these diverse modes of being, the animals in the full range of their diversity belong within our conscious human world in a special manner. A few years ago, Joanne Lausch wrote a book concerned with the smaller animals, namely, the insects. The title, *The Voice of the Infinite in the Small* (1999), indicates that even those living forms that we are least attracted to have their own special role in the grand design of the universe. They speak to us and must not be slighted or treated with contempt. If we assault them with chemical sprays, they will mutate and defeat us time after time.

—"Loneliness and Presence," in *Evening Thoughts*, 33–34

CELEBRATING THE UNIVERSE

As humans we come into being as an integral part of this million-fold diversity of life expression. Earlier peoples celebrated the whole of the universe in its integrity and in its every mode of expression. From the moment of awakening our conscious-ness, the universe strikes wonder and fulfillment throughout our human mode of being. Humans and the universe were made for each other. Our experience of the universe finds festive expres-sion in the great moments of seasonal transformation, such as the dark of winter, the exuberance of springtime, the warmth and brightness of summer, the lush abundance of autumn. These are the ever-renewing moments of celebration of the universe, moments when the universe is in some depth of communion with itself in the intimacy of all its components.

Even with this comprehensive presence of the universe to itself and to its varied components, there is a challenging, even a threatening aspect experienced in every component. Each indi-vidual life-form has its own historical appearance, a moment when it must assert its identity, fulfill its role, and then give way to other individuals in the ever-renewing processes of the phe-nomenal world. In our Western tradition, this passing of our own being is experienced as something to be avoided absolutely. Because we are so sensitive to any personal affliction, because we avoid any threats to our personal existence, we dedicate ourselves to individual survival above all else. In the process of extending the limits of our own lives, we imperil the community of life systems on the planet. This leads eventually to failure in fulfilling our own proper role within the larger purposes of the universe.

Rather than become integral with this larger celebration-sacrificial aspect of the universe, we have elected to assert our personal human well-being and survival as the supreme value. For us, here in the Western world, the human becomes the basic norm of reference for good and evil in the universe. All other modes of being become trivial in comparison. Their reality and value are found in their use relationship to our own well-being. In this context we lose the intimacy that originally we had with the larger community of life. We are ourselves only to the extent of our unity with the universe to which we belong and in which alone we discover our fulfillment. Intimacy exists only in terms of wonder, admiration, and emotional sympathy when beings give themselves to each other in a single psychic embrace, an embrace in which each mode of being experiences its fulfillment.

—"Loneliness and Presence," in *Evening Thoughts*, 34–35

OUR RELATIONS WITH ANIMALS

Although this intimacy exists with the stars in the heavens and with the flowering forms of Earth, this presence of humans with the other members of the animal world has a mutual responsiveness unknown to these other modes of being throughout the universe. Our relation with the animals finds its expression especially in the amazing variety of benefits they provide for us in their guidance, protection, and companionship. Beyond these modes of assistance, they provide a world of wonder and meaning for the mind—beauty for the imagination. Even beyond all these, they provide an emotional intimacy that is unique, that can come to us from no other source. The animals can do for us, both physically and spiritually, what we cannot do for ourselves or for each other. These more precious gifts they provide through their presence and their responsiveness to our inner needs. . . .

At such moments the human venture achieves its validation in the universe, and the universe receives its validation in the human. The grand expression of wonder, beauty, and intimacy is achieved. As Henri Frankfort, an archaeologist, observed, in the ancient Near East the various modes of being of the universe were addressed as "thou" rather than "it." "Natural phenomena were regularly conceived in terms of human experience, and human experience was conceived in terms of cosmic events." As humans, we awaken to this wonder that stands before us. We must discover our role in this grand spectacle.

Recovery of Western civilization from its present addiction to use, as our primary relation to each other and to the world about us, must begin with the discovery of the world within, the world of the *psyche* as designated by the Greeks, a word translated by the term *anima* in the Latin world or by the term *soul* in the English world. The term *anima* is the word used to identify a living or animated or ensouled being from the earliest period in European thought. While the word *soul* has been abandoned by scientists lest it compromise the empirical foundations of their study, the reality of the thought expressed remains forever embedded in the very language that we use. The term *animal* will forever indicate an ensouled being.

—"Loneliness and Presence," in *Evening Thoughts*, 39–40

MUTUAL INDWELLING

This interior world of the psyche—the anima, the soul, the spirit, or the mind—provides the basis for that interior presence that we experience with each other throughout the world of the living. Simply in their physical dimensions, things cannot occupy the same space while remaining their individual selves. This mutual indwelling in the same psychic space is a distinctive capacity of the transmaterial dimension of any living being. Not only can two psychic forms be present to each other in the same psychic space, but an unlimited number of forms can be present. Indeed the entire universe can be present, for as Thomas Aquinas tells us, "The mind in a certain manner is all things." Even so, this inner presence, while distinct from, is not separate from, the outer experience. This capacity for indwelling each other, while remaining distinct from each other, is a capacity of soul or mind or the realm of the psyche. In this integral realm of both the inner and the outer realms is where we discover our fulfillment.

To reduce any mode of being simply to that of a commodity within the community of existence is a betrayal. While the nonliving world does not have a living soul as a principle of life, each member of the nonliving world does have the equivalent as its inner principle of being. This is an inner form that communicates a power, an enduring quality, and a majesty that even the living world cannot convey. In a more intimate way the nonliving world provides the mysterious substance that transforms into life. Throughout this entire process, a communion takes place that belongs to the realm of spirit. There is a spirit of the mountain, a spirit surely of the rivers and of the great blue sea. This spirit mode has been recognized by indigenous peoples everywhere, also by the classical civilizations of the past where such spirits were recognized as modes of personal presence.

Both to know and to be known are activities of the inner form, not of the outer structure of things. This inner form is a distinct dimension of, not a separate reality from, the visible world about us. To trivialize this inner form, to reduce it to a dualism, or to consider it a crude form of animism is as unacceptable as would be the attribution of the experience of sight to a refinement of the physical impression carried by the light that strikes the eye, or the reduction of the communication inherent in a Mozart symphony to vibrations of the instruments on which it is played.

One of the most regrettable aspects of Western civilization is the manner in which this capacity for inner presence to other modes of being has diminished in these past few centuries. While the full expression of this diminished capacity has come in recent centuries, it is grounded in the deeper tendencies in our cultural traditions to emphasize the spiritual aspect of the human over and against the so-called nonspiritual aspect of the other modes of being.

We might think of ourselves as recovering from the pervasive attitude of Western civilization, which designates the human as a superior mode of being and use as our primary relation with the world about us. We have only begun to realize that we are, precisely in our human mode of being, a single if also an immensely significant component in the great community of existence. We might remember that the reality of our own existence can be validated only in the context of honoring the larger communication that the natural world offers us in terms of wonder for the mind, beauty for the imagination, and intimacy for the emotions. Our longing to experience the sight and presence of wilderness creatures seems to indicate that already we are beginning to experience the loneliness of which Chief Seattle warned.

—"Loneliness and Presence,"
in *Evening Thoughts*, 40–42

12

Musings over a Life

Thomas grew up in a newly industrializing South. His early experience of seeing factories and urbanization change the agrarian nature of the South marked him deeply and remained with him throughout his life. Indeed, when he returned to North Carolina in 1994 he was still dismayed at the rapid development in the area. He spent the last fourteen years of his life there reflecting on what had been lost in its deleterious effect on human communities. He lamented the relentless consumerism and growth evident in the careless destruction of land for malls, oversized houses, and pesticide-maintained golf courses.

His youth in Greensboro had provided the basis for an intimacy with the natural world that he nurtured throughout his life. This is what he described in "The Meadow Across the Creek." The experience of seeing the meadow in all of its beauty on a spring afternoon in May left such an impression on him that over the years this became normative for his thinking. "Whatever preserves and enhances this meadow in the natural cycles of its transformations is good; whatever opposes this meadow or negates it is not good. My life orientation is that simple."

For Thomas this was more than a romantic encounter with nature in its spring beauty. It was an experience that grounded his thinking in the depths of reality. Here was a thriving ecosystem blooming with lilies, redolent with bird song and insect flight.

This complex array of living systems is what inspired Thomas to explore those creative cosmic forces that had birthed this beauty and the creative human forces that would be required to sustain this complexity.

This became a life-long quest to discover the cosmological dimensions of Earth's systems within the vast unfolding of the universe. Our presence within this immensity both in life and in death also fascinated him. He could say with ease that even after death he would be part of the universe.

Moreover, to establish the conditions for nurturing the meadow across the creek he observes that we need to create peace with Earth. Our cosmological understanding of the interconnectedness of Earth—geological, biological, and human—is the basis for a Pax Gaia. This must be dreamt into being, as well as constructed. The power of our imagination to envision a shared future is what lies on the horizon. Berry has provided a way forward into that horizon. As Thomas said in Evening Thoughts: *"We are just discovering that the human project itself is a component of the Earth project, that our intimacy with Earth is our way to intimacy with each other. Such are our foundations for our journey into the future."*

THE MEADOW ACROSS THE CREEK

My own understanding of the Great Work began when I was quite young. At the time I was about eleven years old. My family was moving from a more settled part of a small southern town out to the edge of town where the new house was being built. The house, not yet finished, was situated on a slight incline. Down below was a small creek and there across the creek was a meadow. It was an early afternoon in late May when I first wandered down the incline, crossed the creek, and looked out over the scene.

The field was covered with white lilies rising above the thick grass. A magic moment, this experience gave to my life something that seems to explain my thinking at a more profound level than almost any other experience I can remember. It was not only the lilies. It was the singing of the crickets and the woodlands in the distance and the clouds in a clear sky. It was not something conscious that happened just then. I went on about my life as any young person might do.

Perhaps it was not simply this moment that made such a deep impression upon me. Perhaps it was a sensitivity that was developed throughout my childhood. Yet, as the years pass, this moment returns to me, and whenever I think about my basic life attitude and the whole trend of my mind and the causes to which I have given my efforts, I seem to come back to this moment and the impact it has had on my feeling for what is real and worthwhile in life.

This early experience, it seems, has become normative for me throughout the entire range of my thinking. Whatever preserves and enhances this meadow in the natural cycles of its transformation is good; whatever opposes this meadow or negates it is not good. My life orientation is that simple. It is also that pervasive. It applies in economics and political orientation as well as in education and religion.

What is good in economics is that which fosters the natural processes of this meadow. What is not good in economics is that which diminishes the capacity of this meadow to renew itself each spring and to provide a setting in which crickets can sing and birds can feed. Such meadows, I later learned, are themselves in a continuing process of transformation. Yet these evolving biosystems deserve the opportunity to be themselves and to express their own inner qualities. As in economics, so in jurisprudence and law and political affairs—what is good recognizes the rights of this meadow and the creek and the woodlands beyond to exist and flourish in their ever-renewing seasonal expression even while larger processes shape the bioregion in its sequence of transformations.

Religion too, it seems to me, takes its origin here in the deep mystery of this setting. The more a person thinks of the infinite number of interrelated activities that take place here, the more mysterious it all becomes. The more meaning a person finds in the Maytime blooming of the lilies, the more awestruck a person might be in simply looking out over this little patch of meadowland. It has none of the majesty of the Appalachian or the western mountains, none of the immensity or the power of the oceans, nor even the harsh magnificence of desert country. Yet in this little meadow the magnificence of life as celebration is manifested in a manner as profound and as impressive as any other place I have known in these past many years.

It seems to me that many people had such experiences before we entered into an industrial way of life. The universe, as manifestation of some primordial grandeur, was recognized as the ultimate referent in any human understanding of the wonderful yet fearsome world about us. Every being achieved its full identity by its alignment with the universe itself. With indigenous peoples of the North American continent, every formal activity was first situated in relation to the six directions of the universe, the four cardinal directions combined with the heavens above and the earth below. Only thus could any human activity be fully validated.

The universe was the world of meaning in these earlier times, the basic referent in social order, in economic survival, in the healing of illness. In that wide ambience the Muses dwelled, whence came the inspiration of poetry and art and music. The drum, heartbeat of the universe itself, established the rhythm of dance, whereby humans entered into the entrancing movement of the natural world. The numinous dimension of the universe impressed itself upon the mind through the vastness of the heavens and the power revealed in the thunder and lightning, as well as through the springtime renewal of life after the desolation of winter. Then too the general helplessness of the human before all the threats to survival revealed the intimate dependence of the human on the integral functioning of things. That the human had such intimate rapport with the surrounding universe was possible only because the universe itself had a prior intimate rapport with the human as the maternal source form whence humans come into being and are sustained in existence.

—"The Meadow Across the Creek," in *The Great Work*, 12–14

REFLECTIONS ON DEATH

Berry: Death is integral to the process of life and existence. We are born of others; we survive through others; we die into others. It is part of a total process, a community process, which is what the universe is. It is the world of the living—of birth, life, and death. I think of it like a symphony. There's nothing that happens in time that does not have an eternal dimension. That is, like music, it is played through a sequence of notes or a sequence of time, but must be understood outside time. It must be understood simultaneously. The first note and the last note have to be understood as the simultaneous experience of the melody. And so the whole universe, in a certain sense, is played through in sequence but it also exists outside this sequence.

Mary Judith Ress: But we human beings have tremendous fear of death. What do you think happens after death? Is there a separation? Does the body disintegrate and the soul or spirit continues?

Berry: It is a total process, and the whole being is part of that process. Our disintegration is the disintegration of a certain phase of a person's being. But the whole life process is transcendent to a time process. Therefore birth and death are both contained in the reality of a person's existence.

Ress: Very concretely, where will Thomas Berry be fifty years from now?

Berry: Why, I'll be where I have always been.

Ress: Which is?

Berry: Each of us is as old as the universe and experiences our greater self in the larger story of the universe. So we are as old as the universe and as big as the universe. That is our great self. We survive in our great self. Our particular manifestation is distinct from our universal presence to the total process. We exist eternally in our participation in the universe's existence.

Ress: Is what you're saying different from our yearning for immortality?

Berry: No, it's just a question of how a person thinks about immortality. The universe itself is the comprehensive mode of existence—everything exists in relationship to the universe. Everything participates in everything that happens in the universe. Therefore we never cease to be participants in the universe. Everything we do will have consequences that will go on forever. There is a way in which we exist individually as a dimension of the totality of things and as an influence on everything that to some extent governs what came before us and everything that will come after us.

—Interview by Mary Judith Ress
for the Spanish language magazine
Con-spirando, 1994

SPIRITUALITY AND ECOLOGY

We should be clear about what happens when we destroy the living forms of this planet. The first consequence is that we destroy modes of divine presence. If we have such a wonderful sense of the divine, it is because we live amid such awesome magnificence. If we have such refinement of emotion and sensitivity, it is because of the delicacy and fragrance and indescribable beauty of song, and music and rhythmic movement in the world about us. If we have strength and grow in vigor of body and soul it is because the Earth community challenges us, forces us to struggle to survive; but in the end leads us to a conviction that we live in an ultimately benign universe. But however benign, it must provide that absorbing drama of existence whereby we can experience the full thrill of being alive in a fascinating and unending sequence of adventures.

If we have powers of imagination, these are activated by the magic display of color and sound, of form and movement, such as we observe in the clouds of the sky, the trees and bushes and

flower, the waters and the wind, the singing birds, and movement of the blue whale through the sea.

If we have words to speak and to think and commune with,
words for the inner experience of the divine, words for the intimacies of life; if we have words for telling stories to our children,
words that we can sing with, it is again because of the impres-
sions we have received from the variety of beings about us.

If we lived on the moon, our minds and emotions, our speech,
our imagination, our sense of the divine would be limited to the
lunar landscape.

The change that is taking place on Earth and in our minds is
one of the greatest transformations ever to take place in human
affairs, perhaps the greatest, since what we are talking about is
not simply another historical change or cultural modification
but a shift at a geobiological order of magnitude. We are changing Earth on a scale comparable only to those significant shifts
in the structure of Earth and of life that took place during some
hundreds of millions of years of Earth development.

While such an order of magnitude can produce a paralysis of
thought and action, it can, hopefully, also awaken in us a sense
of what is happening, the scale on which things are happening,
and move us to a vast program of reinhabiting Earth in a truly
human manner.

It could awaken in us an awareness of the need we have for
all the living companions that we have with us here on our
homeland planet. To lose any of these splendid companions is to
diminish our own lives.

To learn how to live graciously together would make us worthy
of this unique beautiful blue planet that was prepared for us over
some billions of years, a planet that we should give over to our
children with the assurance that this great community of the living will nourish them, guide them, heal them and rejoice in them
as it has nourished, guided, healed, and rejoiced in ourselves.

—"Spirituality and Ecology," selection from a sermon delivered by
Thomas Berry at the Cathedral of St. John the Divine,
New York City, Sunday, November 8, 1981

COSMOLOGY OF PEACE

My proposal is that the cosmology of peace is presently the basic issue. The human must be seen in its cosmological role just as the cosmos needs to be seen in its human manifestation. This cosmological context has never been clearer than it is now, when everything depends on a *creative resolution of our present antagonisms*. I refer to a *creative resolution of antagonism* rather than to *peace* in deference to the violent aspects of the cosmological process. Phenomenal existence itself seems to be a violent mode of being. Also, there is a general feeling of fullness, bordering on decay, that is easily associated with *peace*. Neither *violence* nor *peace* in this sense is in accord with the creative transformations through which the more splendid achievements of the universe have taken place. As the distinguished anthropologist A.L. Kroeber once indicated: The ideal situation for any individual or culture is not exactly "bovine placidity." It is, rather, "the highest state of tension that the organism can bear creatively."

In this perspective, the present question becomes not the question of conflict or peace, but how we can deal creatively with these enormous tensions that presently afflict our planet. As Teilhard suggests, we must go beyond the human into the universe itself and its mode of functioning. Until the human is understood as a dimension of Earth, we have no secure basis for understanding any aspect of the human. We can understand the human only through Earth. Beyond Earth, of course, is the universe and the curvature of space. This curve is reflected in the curvature of Earth and finally in that psychic curve whereby the entire universe reflects back on itself in human intelligence.

This binding curve that draws all things together simultaneously produces with the inner forces of matter that expansive tension whereby the universe and Earth continue on their creative course. Thus the curve is sufficiently closed to hold all things together while it is sufficiently open to continue its creative emergence into the future. This tenuous balance between collapse and expansion contains the larger mystery of that functional cosmology which provides our most profound understanding of our human situation, even if it does not bring it within reach of our rational processes.

In this context, our discussion of peace might well be understood primarily in terms of the Peace of Earth. This is not simply *Pax Romana* or *Pax Humana*, but *Pax Gaia*, the Peace of Earth, from the ancient mythic name for the planet.

We can understand this Peace of Earth, however, only if we understand that Earth is a single community composed of all its geological, biological, and human components. The Peace of Earth is indivisible. In this context, the nations have a referent outside themselves for resolving their difficulties.

—"The Cosmology of Peace," in
The Dream of the Earth, 219–20

EVENING THOUGHTS

Delivered at the Millennium World Peace Summit
of Religious and Spiritual Leaders, August 2000

During these past few days much has been accomplished to advance the cause of peace by our discussions and simply by our being with each other. We learn to trust and admire each other and to share with each other the traditions we represent.

This evening I suggest that we continue this presence to each other by looking beyond ourselves to the larger universe we live in. If it were convenient, I would suggest that we go outside this building, that we go beyond all the light and noise of the city, and look up at the sky overarching Earth. At this time in the evening, we would see the stars begin to appear as the sun disappears over the horizon. The light of day gives way to the darkness of night. A stillness, a healing quiet, comes over the landscape.

It is a moment when some other world makes itself known, some numinous presence beyond human understanding. We experience the wonder of things as the vast realms of space overwhelm the limitations of our human minds. At this moment, as the sky turns golden and the clouds reflect the blazing colors of evening, we participate in the intimacy of all things with each other.

Parents hold their children more closely and tell stories to the children as they go off into dreamland, wonderful stories of times gone by, stories of the animals, of the good fairies, adventure stories of heroic wanderings through the wilderness, stories of dragons threatening to devour the people, and of courageous persons who saved our world in perilous times. These final thoughts of the day are continued in the minds of children as even in their sleep they begin to dream of their own future, dreams of the noble deeds that would give meaning to their lives. Whether awake or asleep, the world of wonder fills their minds, the world of beauty fills their imaginations, the world of intimacy fills their emotions.

When we look back over our own lives, we realize that whatever of significance we have achieved has been the fulfillment of earlier thoughts and dreams that sustained us when we encountered difficulties through the years.

Beyond the dreams of our personal future, there are the shared dreams that give shape and form to each of our cultural traditions. Because this other world cannot be explained by any technical or scientific language, we present this other world by analogy and myth and story. Even beyond childhood, this is the world of the human mind.

So tonight as we look up at the evening sky, with the stars emerging against the fading background of the sunset, we think of the mythic foundations of our future. We need to engage in a shared dream experience.

The experiences that we have spoken of as we look up at the starry sky at night, and as, in the morning, we see the landscape revealed as the sun dawns over the earth—these experiences reveal a physical world but also a more profound world that cannot be bought with money, cannot be manufactured with technology, cannot be listed on the stock market, cannot be made in the chemical laboratory, cannot be reproduced with all our genetic engineering, cannot be sent by e-mail. These experiences require only that we follow the deepest feelings of the human soul.

What we look for is no longer the *Pax Romana,* the peace of imperial Rome, nor is it simply the *Pax Humana,* the peace among humans, but the *Pax Gaia,* the peace of Earth and every living being on Earth. This is the original and final peace, the peace granted by whatever power it is that brings our world into being. Within the universe, the planet Earth with all its wonder is the place for the meeting "of the divine and the human.

—"Evening Thoughts," *Evening Thoughts,* 137–41

Appendix A

Morningside Cathedral

by Thomas Berry

*After attending the Winter Solstice
at the Cathedral of St. John the Divine*

We have heard in this Cathedral
Bach's Passion
The Lamentations of Jeremiah
Ancient experiences of darkness over the earth
Light born anew
But now, darkness deeper than even God
Can reach with a quick healing power
What sound,
What song,
What cry appropriate
What cry can bring a healing
When a million-year rainfall
Can hardly wash away the life-destroying stain?
What sound?
Listen—earth sound
Listen—the wind through the hemlock
Listen—the owl's soft hooting
in the winter night
Listen—the wolf—wolf song
Cry of distant meanings
woven into a seamless sound
Never before has the cry of the wolf
expressed such meaning
On the winter mountainside
Morningside
This cry our revelation
As the sun sinks lower in the sky
Over our wounded world

The meaning of the moment
And the healing of the wound
Are there in a single cry
A throat open wide
For the wild sacred sound
Of some Great Spirit

A Gothic sound—come down from the beginning of time
If only humans could hear
How see the wolf as guardian spirit
As saviour guide?
Our Jeremiah, telling us,
not about the destruction of
Jerusalem or its temple
Our Augustine, telling us,
not about the destruction of Rome and civilization
Our Bach,
telling us not about the Passion of Christ in ancient times,
But about the Passion of Earth in our times?
Wolf—our Earth, our Christ, ourselves.
The arch of the Cathedral itself takes on the shape
Of the uplifted throat of the wolf
Lamenting out present destiny
Beseeching humankind
To bring back the sun
To let the flowers bloom in the meadows,
The rivers run through the hills
And let the Earth
And all its living creatures
Live their
Wild,
Fierce,
Serene
And Abundant life.

An Appalachian Wedding

by Thomas Berry

Written for the wedding of Paul Winter and Chez Liley

Look up at the sky
the heavens so blue
the sun so radiant
the clouds so playful
the soaring raptors
woodland creatures
meadows in bloom
rivers singing their
way to the sea
wolfsong on the land
whalesong in the sea
celebration everywhere
wild, riotous
immense as a monsoon
lifting an ocean of joy
then spilling it down over
the Appalachian landscape
drenching us all
in a deluge of delight
as we open our arms and
rush toward each other
all of us moved by that vast
compassionate curve
that brings all things together
in intimate celebration
celebration that is
the universe itself.

Notes

Notes to the Introduction

1. Sections of this Introduction are adapted from the Teilhard Study: John Grim and Mary Evelyn Tucker, "Thomas Berry: Reflections on His Life and Thought," *Teilhard Studies* 61 (Fall 2010).

2. John Cobb, preface to *The Christian Future and the Fate of Earth* by Thomas Berry, ed. Mary Evelyn Tucker and John Grim (Maryknoll, NY: Orbis Books, 2009), xi.

Notes to Chapter 3

1. Lynn Margulis and Dorion Sagan, *Microcosmos: Four Billion Years of Microbial Evolution* (Berkeley: University of California Press, 1997), 191.

2. Pierre Teilhard de Chardin, *The Human Phenomenon*, trans. Sarah Appleton-Weber (East Bourne, East Sussex: Sussex Academic Press, 1999), 3.

3. Henry David Thoreau, *Walking: A Little Book of Wisdom* (New York: HarperCollins, 1994), 19.

Notes to Chapter 4

1. Nicholas Black Elk, *Black Elk Speaks, as told through John G. Neihardt* (Lincoln: University of Nebraska Press, 2000 [originally published in 1932]), 35; and Raymond J. De Mallie, ed., *The Sixth Grandfather: Black Elk's Teachings Given to John Neihardt* (Lincoln: University of Nebraska Press, 1984), 133.

2. *Book of Rites, Li Chi*, Book IV, Section I, part 11, "The Yueh Ling," trans. James Legge (New Hyde Park, NY: University Books, 1967), 257.

Notes to Chapter 5

1. Thomas Aquinas, *Summa Contra Gentiles*, 2.45.10.

2. The Forum on Religion and Ecology is located at http://fore. research.yale.edu/.

Notes to Chapter 6

1. Pierre Leroy, ed., *Letters from My Friend, Teilhard de Chardin* (New York: Paulist Press, 1976), 137 (italics added).

2. Tung Chung-shu quoted in Wm. Theodore de Bary, et al. *Sources of Chinese Tradition* (New York: Columbia University Press, 1960), 179.

3. Ibid., 530

4. Ibid.

5. Yao tien 22 in Bernhard Karlgren, *The Book of Documents* (Stockholm: Museum of Far Eastern Antiquities, 1950), 5.

6. Mary Lelia Makara, ed. and trans., *Hsiao Ching* (New York: St. John's University Press, 1961), chap. 7.

7. Wm. Theodore de Bary, et al., *Sources of Japanese Tradition* (New York: Columbia University Press, 1958), 383–84.

8. Galen Fisher, "Nakae Toju: The Sage of Omi," *Transactions of the Asiatic Society of Japan* (1908), 64.

Notes to Chapter 10

1. Norman Myers, "The Biodiversity Crisis and the End of Evolution, *The Environmentalist* (1996): 37–47.

Notes to Chapter 11

1. Henri Frankfort et al., *Before Philosophy* (Chicago: University of Chicago Press, 1946), 12.